JEANS/genes

JEANS/genes

Tawny "Mae" Harris

iUniverse, Inc.
New York   Bloomington

JEANS/genes

Copyright © 2010 by **Tawny "Mae" Harris**

iUniverse books may be ordered through booksellers or by contacting:

iUniverse
1663 Liberty Drive
Bloomington, IN 47403
www.iuniverse.com
1-800-Authors (1-800-288-4677)

ISBN: 978-1-4401-8872-5(pbk)
ISBN: 978-1-4401-8873-2(ebk)

Printed in the United States of America

iUniverse rev. date: 2/3/2010

Dedicated to:

Loyal Dedication
MacYullee
&
Joy

THE

SOURCE

Contents

JESUS "prays on" the Mount of Olives painted with teeth

I. THE SOURCE

This is *not* a curious, mysterious children's storybook. *Beware*, I have warned you. I can't believe why this chosen will, task has seeked me out, "placed on", burdening, taxing my shoulders, physique.

"Take this cup from me Jesus", *Jeans/genes*. The names and places have been changed to protect the innocent and the guilty.

I obey His command rewriting the amateur Living "Bible on" despite unknown, expletive repercussions: ex communication from my belovéd Episcopal Church, Hebrew Tabernacle, and exclusion, ostracization from humanity, society. Losing respect of the elders, members of the Church, and, termination, firing from my livelihood, job, Shop-a-Lot #666, #999 is foreseen, inevitable.

What would I *not* do for Jesus Christ!! He has saved my life too many times over and over again explicitably. God has put me through all this hell – He knew I would write about it one day – my testimony. I am the Creator, The Communion. I AM THAT I AM. God is the Editor, and, the mistakes belong in the book of *Jeans/genes* as veins in faulty marble.

The Holy Trinity, GODHEAD – Father, Son and Holy spirit, Ghost gathered as One are desparately, hungrily needed to give me the strength to "carryon."

This journal, literature, private, personal documentation, autobiography is yours for the asking. Thank you for reading my book.

GOD is controller, ruler of a mighty universe. If He can set the stars and moons in the "everlasting on" Heavens; surely, He can handle your extreme lives, problematic circumstances.

GOD is everything to me – every brain cell, eyesight, hearing, miracle, *gene* atom, molecule, function, memory. All is His.

"Every "hair on" your head is counted, and, mine is wearing thin. Patience and LOVE are virtues. What would I do without this Man, being? I could *not* "live on" deprived of His gracious, air, breath, "eggingon" in this vast, vacilliating world.

GOD's tireless guidance, meticulous, expertised beauty of His exquisite "creation on" Earth reveals, shows the grand artistic nature of His infinite wisdom and mercy. DO NOT let me catch you turning, reversing the letters G-O-D to D-O-G of my Lord.

Jeans are "woven on" sewing machines, apparatuses, needles of our times by industrious, hard-working fingers of arduous, skillful souls of His making.

"Sew on". . .

His meaningful, neverending forgiveness, grace "lives on", "forever on" in our bodies, hearts, minds, thoughts, and spirits.

God has a sense of humor, personality, and, the understanding, concepts, ideas of Him need to be updated, revolutionized, modernized. Technically speaking, God's #1 priority are people, human beings, craven mortals.

All I have to say is . . . Pray your _____ off!

In all honesty,

yours very truly,

Tawny "Mae" Harris

"Ask on". . .

"Seek on". . .

"Knock on". . .

"Praise on". . .

"Believe on". . .

"Beseech on". . .

"Love on". . .

What plane are "we on"?

Shape up or ship out.

The Lord, Jesus be with me and with Thy spirit.

Rebuke the devil, oh my soul, and he will flee.

Praise the Lord !!!

Bless us & keep us, oh my Father.

Pardon us & forgive us.

Be with us forever & ever.

We give thanks to you, oh Lord. It is meet & right so to do at all times & all places to give thanks to the Lord, our God, our heavenly Father. Help me to *always* Bless you, God, Jesus Christ, & the Holy Spirit.

Cast the spirit in everyone's hearts, soul, mind, thoughts, body, & spirit.

Help us to LOVE the Lord, our God, the giver of life. Let no mean thing come into our hearts. We lift our hearts up to Thee, Oh, God, Thy Countenance & Redeemer.

Lord, grant us all loving-kindness, hope, faith, trust, joy, glory, & strength. May all glory be yours!

Angels watching over us

night and day

day and night.

In the name of the Father, Son, & Holy Ghost, Spirit.

Blesséd Trinity!

Oh, Lord, keep us happy & safe, protected under Jesus's wings In God's Name I pray.

--Ask on.—

--Seek on.—

--Knock on.—

--Praise on.—

A BETTER PLACE

A better place would be:
A paradise full of sun.
Turquoise colored water.
Butterflies having fun.

Waterfalls flowing refreshment.
Flowers growing free.
Reflection of a red jeweled
    cruise ship
Waving "hello" in the sea.

No thoughts of ghastly serpents,
Sharks searching the shore.
All beauty & safety
Would always be the norm.

Thankfulness & grateful.
Praising the above
Always acknowledging the Creator
In y our paradise of LOVE.

JESUS

I was sent for a reason.
I know not what it is.
He is the Man of the season.
The bells ring aloud for Him.

I feel so little & small.
Not worth an ant's weight.
Having to "hangon" & call.
The Holy & mysterious date.

My body is solid as a rock.
My spirit is so weak.
Will I ever see that pearly
    gate's lock?
Will I even get to peek?

Heaven is worth far more
Than my sinful soul can tell.
It is real or is it folklore?
The Bible expresses it will.

We travel blindly in faith.
Not seeing but believing laid.
No matter how nearly our
    hearts weigh.
All our debts have been paid.

No test too many to be with
    you, Lord, Jesus.
I know you art with me
    during the storm.
I cannot see you blinded
    by rage.
Jailed by bondage inside my

    cage alarmed.

HOPE

We look at LIFE at all our
tremendous mistakes and such. . .
"You loveth much who
forgiveth much."

We lick our wounds from
the roads we're paved. . .
"Only scarred lives can
    really save."

We bide our time till we depart. . .
"Jesus can only abide in
    humble hearts."

We should watch how we act
and what we say. . .
"Pride bars the way."

Honor your Heavenly Father
& Bless Thee . . . "Win souls for Me."

Drink of His cup. . ." When thy
Mother & Father forsake thee,
I will lift Thee up."

Fertilize your ground with prayer.
Water it with LOVE. Deep roots
Make common sense. Carry me,
please . . . "Footprints," a dove.

THE JOURNEY

Higher, oh higher we climb
Looking "down on" the snow
Blanketing the mountaintops
On the peaks far below.

The higher we ascend
The pressure gets greater
Our souls cannot depend
"Solely on" ourselves now or later.

Rungs beneath our feet
Blend as one ladder
Stairway to where it leads
Faltering footsteps cry sadder.

Never seen where it leads
Testing tougher it seems
Heavenward all the way
'Till death as a team.

'Till death do us part
Our group is determined
Loyal from the start
Men, women, and children.

PROTECTION

Once upon a time, there was a littliest angel whom was given so many blessings to spread per God. Her quota was 37 blessings per this special particular flight.

She Blesséd the boy with a broken leg whom was on crutches to walk. She Blesséd the girl whose precious dolly was misplaced to find it, and, she Blesséd countless families to turn to Jesus for their salvation. Thirty-six and one-half times she shared God's blessings.

Ariana came across a baby who had pneumonia. She only had ½ blessing left and she needed a whole one to save the child's life; so, she left one of her wings.

The wind heard of this adversity for she struggled to no avail to fly. Angels from everywhere came to Ariana's aid and they all lined-up for their next assignments.

SECRET OF SOULS

He makes me believe I AM the only one.
That stole my heart and fled. Maker of the entire universe. Sought me
    out and led.

Brought me to a whole new dimension in life.
One of loving kindness and gratitude.
Consideration and understanding.
Such a gracious and merciful Dude.

That is invisable to the touch.
Yet seen within the hearts.
We know He loves us eternally,
"everlasting on".
We all play our human sacrificial parts.

In the mosaic of His Mind.
Every individual stone is important.
Making Christianity work.
Spreading His Word omnipotent.

Humbly singing, kneeling, bowing.
Your special Place is praised.
Magnified with awe.
All His children's voices raised.

His promises He has kept.
His honor I respect, obeyeth.
Sinners all express His Name.
SECRET souls, joyfully saith.

SONG

I'll be up there one day
You know you broke my heart
I miss you so much
Why did you have to depart?

I blindly look out the window
Don't know what I AM thinking
    I'll see
Maybe, it's the return of the Jedi
or Jesus coming after me.

Refrain: I've been waiting for this day all of my life – Jesus coming after me

I peek twice in the mirror
My hair done up so fine
Waiting patiently for my Man
The One who makes me shine.

Glowing like a Christmas candle
Reverent like a Catholic priest
Shooting like a star from Heaven
quick as a nightly thief.

Refrain: I've been waiting for this day all of my life – Jesus coming after me.

I made passionate love to Him and never physically touched Him in
    the flesh.

GOD

Thou He works in mysterious ways
Ways too Holy to conceive
You know He is Almighty, Merciful
Prayfully, I believe.
Make our faith stronger everyday
Ever closer get us to you
Sustain us with your hopeful rays
Your sunshine beaming through.
We could not do it without you
Our steps are feeble and weak
Lift us up with your mighty
strength
Till we are cheek-to-cheek.

Keep us enwrapped within you, Lord
Les' we stumble and fall
Help us always Bless your Name
When you beacon and call.

Jesus! We thank you for being there
Quick to calm and sooth
Wipe away our tears and then
With you we'll never lose.

When will these voices go away?
    When I do.
If I go, Where will I dwell??
"I promise you many rooms in
My mansion"
"Praise is the devil's death knell."

"THE WORLD"

I AM not scared to death of living.
I AM just scared of living.
It's not that I AM scared to death
    of dying.
I AM just scared of dying.

Because there's life after death,
It's got to be better than this.
The hunger; the pain; the stress;
    the shame.
The struggling; the suffering;
    the fear of the unknown.
The disappointments; the disillusions;
    the evil.
The sacrifices; the dangers;
    the false hope.
The beliefs, the strain;
    the weaknesses.

Jesus is coming again "forever on."
I pray that my dying quest
    for the better.

I AM so nervous about "working on" my bathroom with a 73 old man. The work is too hard & strenuous for me, much less, a man of that age. We talk about sex, how to catch a man, "Fold back the sheets", and, anything else.

Joseph Abraham I can't lift the heavy vanity. I have no other help, and, I will have to call Cross Developers to pick it up. Joseph Abraham is a walking miracle, saint, & Godsend. Lord, Jesus, give *us*, the plumber & I, strength, endurance for another arduous, fulfilling day. He *always* comes right over.

Dear All of second shift, Thank you for helping me with my codes and carts. I appreciate *all* you do. You turned my gray skies into blue ones, and, I AM so proud of you all.

Love,

A Thankful People Greeter

P.S. A wise saying: Success is measured by how high you bounce when you hit rock bottom (with a little help from your friends.)

I AM the source of all unhappiness, sadness.
I AM the source of all free will.
I AM the source of all happiness, joy, gladness.
I AM the source of shielded, yielded kill.
I AM the source of everything, Mary Magdeline.
The source of hearts so true.
You are the conception of *genes*.
Released, relinquished in *jeans*
    of blue.

7th HEAVEN

I dreamed I was on a bus
And, we soared through the sky.
Our first stop was the animals.
I did not question why.

All our past belovéd pets:
Cats and dogs and birds
Tended by kindly shepherds.
What a responsible herd!

Secondly, we stopped at #2.
The sign said quite plainly,
"Forgiveness is divine."

(Thieves and murderers mainly.)

Planting the seed on three.
Acknowledging only out of need.
Made a believer out of me.
He is there for *every* deed.

Four was a moving experience.
These people had hearts of gold.
Always giving themselves to others,
Doing as they were told.

Churchgoers inhabited number five;
Although, they're not perfect,
Prayer dominated their lives.
Hallelujah! There's no serpent!

Sixth floor occupied by such:
Habits and collars and crosses.
Spent their whole life humble.
Counting Blessings and not losses.

Out of the seventh floor,
Came one Holy young man.
You could tell He was on a mission.
Loved traveler of all lands.

He touched her, knelt by her side,
Attired in glowing, majestic robes.
She arose and administered to Him.
He called her Mother Earth, the globe.

ANOTHER DAY

"Lord, God, how are you?
Did you have a bad night?
"Joy cometh in the morning."
I hope you're alright."
"You've *always* taken care of me,
My family and my friends.
You've *always* been there for me.
Hello, how are Thee?!" Amen.

"Is there anything we can do to help?
Alleviate the pain and sorrow,
Dissipate the disappointments,
or just wait until tomorrow."

"Yes, faithful one.
Under protective wings.
One day at a time.
Until your heart sings."
"One place for sure
Needs loyal help to stay
You will be rewarded,
"Have a good day!"

NAMES

Will I see another day?
Will all my dreams come true?
If there is life after death,
Will I have to repay all my dues?

He came so we could live more abundantly.
His sword, the Word, elite.
Chances are if you abide in Him;
He'll humbly wash your feet.

Hymns sing praises up above.
We should *always* give Him thanks.
Continually pray-never cease.
Look to the hilly river banks.
For there our answers lie and wait.
To the hills we search for Him.
The answers to our prayers life
Within our heart's light dim.
He can make the light and dark appear.
Dreams become reality bliss.
Joy is life eternally spent.
On Jesus Christ's loving list.

Dedicated to
Micah, Wrangler
& Jesus Christ, God,
& Holy Spirit

T A R A

II. "TARA"

The house lights briefly flicker, I guess, from power surges. An electrician once told me that was normal. St. Simon told me the ugly but kind electrician blew up smoking a cigarette while under an oxygen mask. He died.

My mind wanders back to Jayden, assistant co-manager, at Shoppe-A-Lot. I AM in love, infatuated with my 27 year old boss. Spring is in the air! God, he's 22 years younger than me, myself.

We cannot become involved because of stupid rules, restrictions from corporate at Shop-a-Lot #666, Shoppe of love. These binding, ignorant commandments of higher-up authority need to "be" broken, changed. I don't know if he would even go out with me, anyway. We might bring our personal problems to work.

Sympathy, CSM, customer service manager "on second" shift – no competition or catfights – just wants to drink beer & play pool with Jayden. What a relief!

Her almost waist length auburn, chocolate cherry, burgundy hair slings, sways side to side when she walks briskly administering, aiding peon, lowly cashiers in perilous, needy appeals. Cash register lights "blink on" demanding, requesting her knowledgable, adept expertise, assistance. Sympathy's Indian features, turquoise jewelry, abrupt approach, final confrontations with irate, disgruntled customers set her apart, favortism unequal, from other floating CMS's.

I AM too old, rich, tired, & weary to fight with the jealousy coveted in the competitive wars vying for the lustful attention of Jayden's uncomparable, untouchable, god-like, rewarding acceptance. I wonder, imagine how he kisses, hound dogging around with his playful, thick tongue hanging out the side of his mouth in jest.

Sympathy's 14 years celebant, because she was abused by her ex-husband who tried to run over her in a car while she was pregnant, beats my suffering celibacy vow once in 13 years.

St. Peter Eater had annoyingly begged me to commit, engage in the undesirable act against my will.

"It's about time you had some." His varicose veins popping "out on" his forehead remind me of a criminal. I can't ride a bicycle but I can swim. He rode my _____ off, and, I faked an orgasim. I appreciated his observance of the welcome turtle on the back porch, stoop when he left.

Jayden excitably, unexpectantly holds up thee visable "fingers on" the crowded front end of Shop-a-Lot regardless of the swarm of unawarded, unknowingly flood of customers in symphathy's and my astonished direction causing my delighted heart to flutter in my throat. This gesture is in regards to a mutually private threesome affair joke.

"Have you ever had a threesome?"

"No."

"I have", casually confiding, blushing.

Jayden waves his hands, panting, as if having a hot flash, indicating the confessed remark is "hot". This reaction pleases, excites me.

Briefly flashing back to the abominable, impulsive occurrence, scene, my commensement, reflection stirs the shameful, embarrassing act of voyeurism. I went first. The other female was rumored to have herpes.. Peter Eater socked it to her with a huge dildo.

Another planned, arranged, naked episode innocently provokes a desparate denial note taped to Peter Eater's front door of his unavailable, empty, vacant rental house:

TOO KINKY – NOT COMING

Peter Eater – a gifted drummer, Elvis Pressley impersonator, Preacher's son excursions, days are over for the time being.

As I redo my list, my thoughts to get everything done, "completed on" my two days off compels me to write. Drinking pineapple soda, relaxing at 11:10 p.m. at night, chilling after a long nap, gives me rested pleasure. Smoking one cigarette after another, sucking in flavor and blowing it out is a habit that, which satisfies rather than produces a guilt trip.

As the crystal ash tray fills-up, I push the dead butts to the side corner. It's 76° degrees in here at the lat day of April.

The refrigerator "kicks on". It is so peaceful & quiet in here. I hear the wall clock ticking. He's gorgeous – big moon greenish-blue hazel eyes that look like a staring deer in floodlights, dopey ears, true character, lanky. He's full of spit & vinegar & dances friskily like a joyful bow-legged country bumpkin, farmer. Jayden is constantly "staying on" my mind, and, I cannot shake him. I cannot muster or even try." The Spirit is willing but the flesh is weak."

My dreamy state of mind is out there, and, I AM writing the first chapter of my book at a cherry dining room table displaying, exhibiting paisley black/burgundy placemats & brick red runner.

The mahogany parkay flooring looms contemplatively, intentionally luring, enticing me to clean the fabricated "wood on" my hands & knees with a handy wipe cloth & Murphy's oil soap.

Wrangler, my belovéd solid white cat with gold eyes, is contented & "asleep on" the plush emerald green & cornflower blue plaid blanket in the living room. The clock is ticking like a synchronized metronome.

The black iron sconces decorated with engraved hearts lifting-up, beholding one red & one blue wax candle like toy trojan soldiers are "accompanied on" picture hangers either adjacent side of the fluid time piece.

The beat "goes on". . .

9-1-1

(911)

Major! Major! Emergency!!
God, why did you let this happen to us – to unite our country, U.S.A. as one.
Do the kamikazes believe that suicide will bring, lift them to a higher plane, level? I believe they go to hell & have to start all over again. If they bomb, touch our statue of liberty, gift from France, we will really "be" furious!

> Signing off,
> Gypsy sky
> (Azul Celeste)

I AM pissed off at the world, and, I will tell you why:

a.) Alison Tahiti, Judge Wholesome Tahiti's adopted genetic son, offspring "knocked on" the glass sliding den doors scaring my startled brother, Micah half to death. He wanted Micah to suck his huge erection, "hard on" off. Alison is not even gay. Micah denied the promiscuous act, "I don't want to run our friendship". It was not the time or the place since I was laid-up in the Zion, Egypt hospital with a ruptured, exploded appendix. Alison, sacred fame, has been promoted to the capitol, Tawaiin, Egypt. We are losing a good tax collector.

b.) "Tara" as in the GONE WITH THE WIND saga – Atlanta bursting into raging, fierce flames – Please do not burn down my shrine, temple, Bethany Home – it is for your sake. Gold, Frankincense, & Myrrh are not good enough gifts. I owe you my life!

c.) God took away my Lord, Jesus Christ, my Rabboni, my teacher, and, I know not where He's laid, where to find Him.

d.) *Why* does God let Satan do these things to us? I don't know. We are not pons in a game of chess. I have seen God in a dream. He is a solid granite stone statue & He is not very happy with the world.

e.)   Don't ever sign, write Merry "X-mas on" my Christmas cards. I AM tired, fed-up, General God, with this devastation, trash, corruption, war! Don't piss an Aquarius off! Blow wind blow! Gas prices! Cigarette prices! Cost of living! I can hear St. Jude's voice, "calm down, Mae, calm down.

P.S. TAKE IT   Signing off,

"OUT ON" the ants!

"You need to   Gypsy sky

"be" in Harlem."   (Azul Celeste)

THE CORNER OF CORNUCOPIA
& EVERLIVING STREET

Capturing sensations surrounding me, absorbing them through my pores, and, filing them in my mind while solely trancing along. . .

Walking down a usually desolate street, but dangerously close to activity, I nonchalantly glance into a carpet distributor's window taking notice of the reflection of my burnt orange suede coat, lined with silk, which is my symbol of belovéd autumn or here it 'tis fall.

Crossing the street to an unoccupied swing in the abandoned school yard, I perch to admire the archaic fantasy – an adoration of mine – an old gray house. If you did not look close enough, you would think it was wood; but, it is termite defensive Brick-gray brick!

My enhancing state of feelings wanders around the occupants, the Greece sisters, whom I have never seen stir, come in or out, or peek forth from the six-story windows with curtains of yellowed and printed lace. The mysterious eyes of the house stare-out over a concrete porch in which steps, of approximately eight, stomp up to the solid wood doors.

Swinging slightly higher trying to kick a branch I never quite hit, I take notice of the front yard, proportionally small to the two-story dream; but, I decide that the black iron, speared, knight-hooded fence surrounding the house makes up for the yard. Over the bushes, I estimate that it must be about four-thirty for the women from the office building are revving their motors to go home.

Cosmetic, yes, there is a cosmetic office in there. It just seems to interrupt the whole thing.

Slowing the swing down to a halt, I shuffle my boots in the dust, cautiously getting up and stooping to pick up my Repetoire, Bach Inventions, and whatever else is in the pile, and squeeze through the privet hedge, not forgetting that the climax of this castle is "placed on" the side. Sure, I AM just making sure that it is still there; still exists. Ah, there it is, the balcony. The also gray brick, pronounced yet unpronounced, balcony jutting out somewhere between the first and second floors. Relieved and satisfied, I continue on" my way to my unpracticed piano lessons.

Home is where the heart is.

There's no place like home – jiggety-jog! I LOVE "Tara". It's taken a lot of hard work, interior, exterior decorating, and is dedicated as a shrine to my Mother, Loyal Dedication, and Jesus Christ.

With love,

Tawny "Mae" Harris

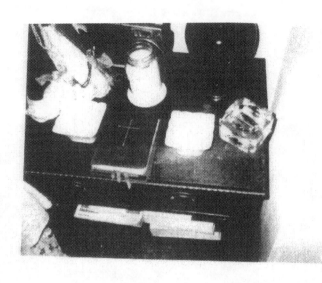

dedicated to:

Brenda Jean

Portugal

&

LOVERS Jane

Pearly

Whites

III. PEARLY WHITES

I have to go to the dentist office today to get my teeth cleaned at 12 noon. It is 0905. I've been up since 6 A.M. drinking coffee & eating BBQ chicken.

The meter reader startles me as he rounded the house. "Mammy, Wonderful Strength, I can't keep my door shut & locked all the time." I keep watch for my cat, wrangler, through the black scrolled door; but, anyone could quickly walk-in.

My mind wanders back, as I accidently light two cigarettes, to a meter reader I once knew, St. Peter Eater. He was tall, dark, & lanky and would not take "No!" for an answer. It was easier to give-in to sex than to fight with him. He begged, pleaded, "suck me".

The dentist & the needles wrack, fray all of my nerves; even though , I AM fond of the dentist himself. Dr. Congeniality goes out of his way to comfort, console you; but, he *always* finds a cavity.

"Well, Dr. Congeniality, I really don't like coming here".

"Well, you know, Mae, I really don't like going to Shop-a-Lot". The smart, sarcastic retort silences me; as, I open my mouth for the drilling.

The cat comes sauntering in, and, I really have to read by books – the Bible & "How To Become a Prayer Warrior," take a hot bath,

& wash my dirty, oily hair. The whole sky looks like it could cry any minute.

Revealing my secret to Gracie Bathsheba, eating breakfast, which is our dinner after working third shift, she doesn't seem amazed, taken back by the hidden remark.

"I'd like to go to hear Jayden play his guitar at the Lavender Forever Church."

"Oh, maybe, I could go & sing."

"No, you wouldn't like to sing in that big church."

The choir, chorus is excellent, flautless. She's good, thinks she can sing: but, she's no match for the Lavender Forever ensemble, group of Angelic raised voices – tenors, sopranos & pianists. I don't want her following me around & embarrasing me; even though, her artistic music degree has paid-off.

Wrangler jumps up and "lays on" my notebook. I kiss her affectionately & continue to write.

Anyway, who would want a fat hog singing in their church. (What an awful & cruel thought.) Gracie has monopolized the services of The Amazing Grace Marines singing soprano, being the "control freak" she is. I want to be left alone in this contemplated endeavor. I want it to be a romantic, pleasant surprize.

Having plenty of time to say, rehearse my weekly rote prayers, I sigh. Praying just keeps my life running, going smoother; and, of course, makes Satan so mad. I expect a sword of hatred to plunge thru me at anytime.

That's why I need the protection of the Lord, Jesus Christ, His grace, mercy, & LOVE to live fruitfully, abundantly another day. The damn devil can't get me!

I refrain from kissing, caressing my sleeping Wrangler "again on" her soft, furry white head. She is residing, resting peaceably beside me "on the dining room table" where I perch my butt most of the time. I can see the constantly, industrious neighbor's, the Islam house, behind the delapidated, unpainted fence wall. My Angel statue & Hummingbird garden flag mesmorizes me with nature's delight.

My concrete bird bath is frequented with blue jays, robins, & bright, scarlet red cardinals. It is so delightfully funny to watch them stick their feathery bodies in the dirty rain water and shake.

Thinking to myself, I can't wait to read this addition, excerpt of my book to my belovéd friend, Joy. She is a good listener, kind friend, and avid, strenuous workaholic.

The visit to the dentist's office wasn't really that bad; in fact, it was fairly good, painless. There's something about cleaning your teeth that makes you want to reveal your whole life history.

After three root canals, two crowns, gum treatment, and numerous fillings, I can dish-out, relate some competitive stories, experiences.

Babylon is a sweetheart, dental hygienist, whom actually enjoys her job, career picking, scraping plaque off of people's, patient's teeth. The first two root canals I encountered, I almost "overdosed on" 4 demoral & 15 tylenol. Waking at 0730, I sincerely thought I would call-in to work when everyone arrived there at 0800 hours. The phone awakened me at 0815. It was my macho boss, Pontious Pilot, calling me from our trucking company, Camel Carriers.

"No, I won't be in today. It hurteth so bad."

My 80 year old Aunt Abundance is beckoned to my rescue of retrieving more addictive demoral & chicken soup.

I get a phone call about 1 p.m.; it's Pontious. "Don't you dare tell anyone I called you; but, are you alright?"

"I'll be there tomorrow." Click.

After a protocol trip to the Personnel Office for uncontrollable crying because of the excrutionary pain, and not calling in, Goodness, personnel director, manager was very understanding. Pounding my "fist on" her desk crying unintentionally "where's my milk shake?!" I AM sure provoked startled emphathy. Where was my Mom when I needed her?! Her passing away, dying months before this painful, resentful catastrophe. Missing one day of work was blown out of proportion.

The receptionists, the girls, at Dr. Congeniality's dentist office are drop dead gorgeous. Competing with their good looks & friendly personalities will never happen. Joash, her bright beautiful smile of straight white teeth," I AM worried about you, Mae."

"SO AM I." Atholiah had a baby girl & hard labor. Portugal, with her dark black eyes lined with white eyeliner, had a radiant, calm smile, meticulous style. She's perfect. Ner always held my hand while I shut, closed my eyes when numbing needles pricked my gums.

All I have to say, Dr. Congeniality has the most lovable congenial horse stable in the town of Zion, Egypt. I cannot say enough about them! Joram visited the Holy Land & briefed me during the months & $700 worth of a fight against gingivitis. She even got to ride a two humped, real camel. she impressed & entertained me during those deep, dark, depressing months of toil, and, suddenly died. Joram is terribly missed & no one can fill her shoes or ever replace her. My heart went-out to that lively dentist office & I grieved along with them. We had lost a precious soul mate.

During a surgical removal of two back teeth, one rotten and the other broke-off at the gum, a remembered & comical episode occurred. In the middle of the procedure, I sit straight-up, stance, stretch my arms in cheerleader fashion, position, "Break!" and march outside to smoke. We still laugh about that impromptu occurance.

"You're the 3rd chapter in the book. You ought to be flattered."

"Be nice to her! She's writing a book!" Babylon, the doll baby of the bunch, would exclaim.

Oh my God! crowns-when he determinely drills your teeth down to a pointed nub. Matching the color of the unreal enamel to my imperfect, yellowed teeth, is a disappointment & relief all at the same time; as, the temporary is lodged in between the crevices. Sometimes, the glue won't hold, stick & the repeated, despairing necessity is encountered again. Laughing profusely during the last root canal while listening to the dreadful gurgling of pulling an old man's teeth was unintended & guilt ridden. The back ground noise, sound was scarey. He was having decayed teeth removed & never once complained.

The crying alarm of a small child shot-up my sympathetic nerves. Pulling children's teeth is an admiral feat of a good dentist. They never cry until it's over.

"You have 3 fillings & 2 of them need to be taken care of soon."

"Dr. Congeniality, you're *always* finding what's wrong with my teeth. You should be rich by now!"

"We just find them; we don't make them."

("I would trust Dr. Congeniality with my life.")

He humbly admits he would rather go to Shop-a-Lot, Shoppe of LOVE, than have a shot.

"I'll call for an appointment when I get my schedule in 3 weeks."

After apologizing for my delayed presence of keeping my appointment "on time" due to doctor visits, I "lean on" the desk counter. Hiroshima, Hashimoto tumor (benign) – whatever, & double creatin kidney levels. I proceed home with clean teeth, and, I think I'll eat something & go rake that hedge.

It starts to sprinkle; but, I sweep my driveway, anyway. Miracle left all the grass everywhere when he mowed my yard.

Sitting here & chilling, I hear a knock at the front door. Jumping up, I lock the back door & go to see who it is. (Jayden?!)

"Can I help you?"

He doesn't hear me. I open the blinds.

"Can I help you?"

"I AM Joab Achan. I see the Tru Green "label on" his shirt. Dark black wavy short hair, brown eyes, clean cut – "I'd like to do your lawn."

"I have somebody that does my yard," speaking through the rectangular windows in the door.

"What?"

"I have somebody that does my yard."

"Thank you. Sorry to bother you."

My ears suddenly go deaf.

(Oh, my God! I couldn't go deaf. I couldn't write! It would be from the sense of the eyes only – borderline glaucoma, cataracts forming.

Singing in my head, "Power in the blood, Power in the blood." I can hear Mrs. Acts singing that hymn out of tune, of course; but, she enjoys "making a joyful noise."

The Amazing Grace Marines is a hoot compared to my church, Episcopalian Hebrew Tabernacle.

I have attended this church since kindergarten. We revertly bow to the cross; make the sign of the cross – Father, Son, & Holy Ghost, Spirit; Kneel & stand to sing religiously getting our work-out, exercise; & take communion (Jesus blood) every Sunday. "The bread of life, manna, the cup, blood of salvation."

Joy did a kind, helpful deed driving, carting me to the dentist to get a back molar pulled – crunched – out. I'll never forget it & will never be able to pay back the considerate, thoughtful event. We bought windchimes together.

Lee had just died the week before, and, I was in no mood, shape, or form to undergo a major extraction. Lee, my beautiful, Collie-Husky, was put down, euthanized, her belovéd head in my lap, & carried-off in a body bag. She was 12.

"3-3-4-6-2-5" was commonly heard when analyzing my gum pockets. "This tooth is a 12-infected. It's got to come-out now!"

I think I'll go to my own church this Sunday.

My book is a hit; as, I AM paged to the Ad Office. I know they are going to fire me for writing such an explicit, truthful, matter of fact novel, autobiography. Martha, the bleached blonde strict manager of store #666 says, "Mae, will you sign my book?!"

(Yeah, right!) If you dream, you might as well dream big!

God knew what He was doing when he put me through all this hell. He knew that I would write it down one day.

One critic writes "Pours out her heart & relieves her soul."

("on guard" – not my job, problem- "These people are my #1 priority at Shop-a-Lot. I retort, relay firmly but sheepishly to the ignorant _____, L.P. (loss prevention). Mae is cheap; but, she's not easy. I like it sloppy not slobbery.) She is dating Jayden.

"Pull it out, Dr. Congeniality! Stick those needles in. No 1%, please."

"Feels like a bear chasing you in the woods – adrenalin pumping."

Puked all over myself driving home.

Faith called. "You know your Aunt Abundance is allergic to novacaine."

My cousin called me just in the nick of time.

Mae & Micah:

Tsh Votheth Funeral Home & Rev. Daniel will take care of details as far as Memorial Service & work with you. I know you'll be strong and fine, as I would want.

Get Priest to cater food & for after Memorial Services to come by home. Rev. Daniel will announce it after service. Have finger sandwiches, maybe shrimp, smoked turkey or tenderloin, lemon tarts, nuts, etc. Priest will have suggestions. Have wine, liquor, set-ups, beer, etc. Remember, there are 2 ins. policies to collect on. It will pay mtg., funeral expenses, etc. As far as house, I wouldn't rush any decisions. Take months to decide. We've discussed how if Mae decides she wants to keep it. You may decide to live together, who knows. But, Micah, take your share of dishes, glasses, casseroles, utensils. There's enough to share. The table with the silverware is Micah's. The chest is Mae's. Micah should have all those cookbooks, if he wants. The corner cupboard & the table in the living room he's always wanted. Don't be ugly in sharing.

Take care of each other.

Know I love you very much.

Mom,

Loyal Dedication

She died Feb. 18, 1994, 65 years of age from throat cancer.

Eve, the nurse & I said a beautiful, farewell prayer for her. Rainbow reflections flooded the glass door. I knew she had made it. She had a tear in her eye.

Loyal Dedication before & after throat cancer. Dr. Congeniality's father, Dad found the lesion, hole the size of a quarter in her mouth.

"You have to go to another doctor for this, Loyal." The oral screening proved fatal."

I should have had my two front teeth, knocked down my throat, esophagus. Blow it out your _____. I "AM on" your side. I *love* you! At least I AM not gumming it. Life is a bully. "Are you destined to win souls for me?" Take it one bicuspid at a time. "Chew on", any way. Don't worry-we'll find Him. They will kill Him! Keep Him safe. Jesus Christ "on Calvary" will never happen again.

"Crucify Him! Crucify Him!" haunts, worries me. How did we ever do this before?

When I get up there, I AM going to beat your _____ off! – Loyal Dedication. Don't worry, we had some good times. Just wait till lovable, adorable Peace gets up there – her curled, soft black hair, puppy dog brown eyes. "Mother doesn't know best." She was a brutal, repulsive alcoholic, gambler; "but she was your Mother, Mae." No wonder your sisters, Beautiful Patience, Wisdom, & Abundance would "walk on" the other tracks, "sidewalks on" the way to school. You "get on" my last nerve – piss me off!

"Shut up!" "You shut me up!" You have some good ideas.

I won't say we are better off without you. Brush your teeth! "You were smoking a cigarette." Your Lucky Strike non-filter cancer sticks are still in the refrigerator wrapped in cellaphane, plastic. They are sacred! God, how I hated kissing your chapped, glossed lips – red lipstick every night before going to bed ritually. I love you, anyway. What a horrible way to die. "What are we being punished for?" Drunken rages, arguments, _____ chewings 3 nights a week.

The retort, remark to Tested Curse, "I won't fight your battles for you, Mae." Why not? You're my parent. Why did you leave me the house – to rub my nose in it – the bills, responsibilities of being a single parent. Why didn't Dad, Perseverence, give us more money, help out more? He could afford a lawyer. I don't *deserve* this beautiful, inherited, Blesséd house, home!

"Puppet on" a string." Follow your own heart – wisdom teeth and all. Cremation sucks! I was 36.

signing off,

Gypsy Sky

(Azul Celeste)

P.S. All I want for Christmas is my two front teeth.

With all my *hope*, Tawny "Mae" Harris.

Dearest To Whom It May Concern:

I had spoken to Ms. Russia about using the origin meanings in *"What shall we name the Baby?* in my autobiography dissertations of my book, *Jeans/genes.* It was out of the question – too costly, expensive. She was much too kind to return my telephone call. I had also spoken to a man (God, I wish I could remember his name); he said he didn't have a problem about handwriting the book. I thoroughly enjoyed talking to him. The myths of New York City are so untrue. These two experiences with New Yorkers has proven uplifting & much more than cordial appeal.

The reason I want to hand write the book is because when I was incarcerated for Manic-Depression & paranoid schizorphrenia, I was "placed on" the drug, Lithium. My hands tremored, trembled and my tongue warbled resulting in 80 year old chicken scratching and loss of my admirable, treasured penmanship. The drug cogentin (Benztropin) medicine for Parkinson's disease, was quickly administered and my handwriting was regained, restored. It is not perfect by no means; but, has "lived on" thru 5 nervous breakdowns, an abortion, father of the baby shooting himself, Mother shooting herself in front of my brother & I, etc., etc. 18 individuals short books; an outline, 3 poem examples, excerpts & personal, original artistic work are enclosed. The first 2 chapters are ready to go.

The reason, purpose for writing this book is to save the world, get it ready for Jesus Christ, help frustrated Christians, save devils, satanists, prevent suicide, console mentally ill people, patients to let them know they are not alone in the world, & prevent drug, alcohol, sexual abuse of children.

Of course, paying-off personal bills, debts of myself, and Shop-a-Lot associates, comrads is also dreamed & envisioned.

The names & places have been changed to protect the innocent & the guilty, and graphic sex scenes place my "reputation on" the line, "out on" a limb, & in jeopardy. What reputation?!

I truly hope you will consider my book of *Jeans/genes*, and, please, advise "me on" copyright laws, publication procedures, binding, & estimated costs, expenditures.

Yours very truly,

Tawny "Mae" Harris

I work 3rd shift at Shop-a-Lot. Mornings before noon are the best time to call. I might not make too much sense after that time period. Thank you for your time, expertise, and, I hope to be hearing from you very soon.

THE TOOTH FAIRY

Genetic pool commonly fused as one jeans of confusion, "anyway on".

Arms that graph, grasp.

All we know of LOVE

Is that LOVE is all there is.

It all ends in a confusing laugh.

Here is a list of all the good things

My Mother, Loyal Dedication,

Father, Perseverence brings.

Gifts from Christmases past & gone.

Earned in honor, respect –

Eternally won.

Where did my tooth fairy go?

Round & round, nobody knows.

Under my pillow as I solemnly,

Peacefully slept,

My lost, precious tooth placed,

Secretly kept.

The surprize of a quarter

Lovingly found.

Gingerly seeking, tooth fairy profound.

Joy, I have never been a parent

From the other side of the tracks.

Hitting your son, Baptist, smack

In the mouth,

Silver braces defensively cracked.

Protecting yourself in a teenager

Ranting rage

Busting his braces, preventing decay.

No respect given because you
weren't financially working
All I know is, the threat of
Hitting you disrespectfully lurking.
In those adverse circumstances,
I do not know what I've done.
Baptist is a good boy, inspite,
Your only favorable son.
Methodist, his father, working
His butt off for the misdeed
Was a good disciplinatory
Punishment
Frustrations harsely, emotionally
Freed, relieved.
The dentist consoled, mutually,
In subordinately agreed.
He'd hit his own boys right
In the mouth
This I can't unbelievably,
Shockingly see.

Loyal Dedication:

a.)   stood by our sides through thick and thin in sickness & in health.

b.)   kept the comfortable, spacious home, house running properly, smoothly without upsetting, scaring us with needed repairs.

c.)   wrote the bills at work without rubbing our nose in them.

d.)   good cook, gourmet genius.

e.)   loyally, steadfastly, religiously went to work every single day of her life & made a living as a Real Estate broker & secretary.

f.)   good sense of humor – told some really cool jokes:

There once was this guy who went to a bar & nobody paid any attention to him; so, he went to a barber. "Dye my hair black." He went back to the bar, and, nobody still paid any attention to him. He went back to the barber.

"Put a yellow streak, green streak, purple streak, orange streak, blue streak in my hair." He went back to the bar, and, they're was an old man staring at him." "What's wrong, haven't you ever seen a man before?" "Yeah, I _____ a peacock once, and, I thought maybe you were my son."

There was this lady & she was coming back from her husband's funeral with his cremated ashes in an urn. He was a cheapscate. She stopped at a car dealership & bought a cadillac, then, she proceeded

53

to buy a mink coat at the furiers. She goes home, "Henry, remember that cadillac you always promised me. It's out in the garage." "Henry, remember that fur coat you always promised me. I've got it on!" "Henry, remember that blow job you always wanted." She upturns the urn. Whoosh. She blows his ashes all over the table.

There was this pig farmer, and, this man comes up & wants to buy a pig. The pig farmer picks up the pig, takes it's tail, twirls it around in his mouth," That'll be two dollars." The man said, "How can you weigh a pig that way?"

"You can go up to the house & pay my wife." The man comes back from the house.

"Well, did you get everything straightened-out paying my wife?"

"No, she was too busy weighing the mailman."

g.)   Mom took "us on" really-cool trips: the turquoise blue oceans of the Red Sea, Lamentations; trips to Deuteronomy, Colossians, Egypt where we swam all summer, waded the cool, clean streams where I dropped my lipstick out of my bra in the flowing, running water of the creek, embarrassingly, in front of a friendly stranger. Weep, a friend of Loyal's, witness, her now accountant son, Micah, my brother & I were manning Wisdom's & Humor's, Aunt & Uncle's apartment while they were gone. Haggai jaunts, refreshing apple cider; Jebosite zoo & museum with lovable, adorable family friend, Peace and her cute, black-haired son, Tabor.

Famous artwork, astronomy, arrowheads, archaic relics enlightened our busy day. When Mom, Loyal Dedication frequented the Jebosite zoo at a younger age, the caged ape grabbed-off her sunglasses & threw "SH#T on" her; Hosea/Chronicles lake parties with Maebelle & the Aziahs – boating, water skiing; Mary Poppins & Oliver movies (super califragilistic exipi alidocious); Tibet park-rustic cabins, paddle boats with her drug addicted R.N. nurse friend, Japan, & her 2 daughters, Eternity and China; thoroughbred Hosea horse races.

h.) Good boss, employer to work for – probably the most understanding, lenient boss I had while attending Zion Egypt Community College.

i.) over protective, strict, extremely caring.

j.) probably the best, golden-hearted person you'd ever know.

k.) named 2 streets after my brother & I in a developed apartment complex: Mae Avenue & Micah court.

l.) good, smart business woman; avid, religious book reader.

m.) gave us bar spending money.

n.) put our car "insurance on" her policy to save us money.

o.) devout, renown animal lover.

p.) did without new clothes.

q.) left Micah & I a $5000 insurance policy which I purchased, bought an used azul blue Lumina.

Perseverence:

a.)   great strides, accomplishments in his 84 year lifetime.

b.)   Professor of Mining Engineering at U.K. (United Kingdom).

c.)   ex-Marine Captain.

d.)   2 awesome step Mothers – Pearl & Laughter.

e.)   good, dry sense of wit, humor.

f.)   "stickler on" dates, history.

g.)   good-looking, handsome, bald.

h.)   highly intelligent.

i.)   good, fun times – movies, delicious, expensive dinners, meals – prime rib, martinis – dry, olive up.

j.)   treasured, looked forward to yearly visits – wish I had more time with him – divorced, abandoned when I was 2.

k.)   encouragement – "keep on" plugging."

They both had their own set of teeth – coveted, relished pearly-whites.

All I have to say is,

"Joy on."

Dedicated to:

Beautiful Patience

&

Wonderful Strength

 **taTToo**

IV. TATTOO

Serenity (Serenidad)

Meadow of flowers and butterflies wisps of clouds and clear blue skies
Red vacation cruise in an ocean scene awaiting like a ruby jeweled
queen.

Palm trees and a waterfall

Breezy air and crystal balm

Picturesque enchanted tale

Coyfish and mystic whales.

Wandering through this dream of mine

Whimsical fairies and beauty kind

Island full of carefree bliss

Warm sea breeze and sweet sun-kissed

Set your "sight on" things above

In my paradise of gifted love

Spiritual heights and creation just

Tropical pleasure and relaxing trust.

Bluejeans, tattoos, psychodelic ink
Sparkling genes, chromosomes lined
Chains of fiber, "living on"
Land of prayer, Jesus won.

A touch of Heaven forever mine
Thank you, God, for treasured time.
There are just as many jeans as there are tattoos:

blue jeans

red jeans

white jeans

black jeans

khaki jeans

navy jeans

maroon jeans

ragged, torn jeans

holey jeans

tight jeans

slit jeans

sexy jeans

embroidered jeans

crotchless jeans

dirty jeans

starched jeans

baggy jeans

designer jeans

LEE jeans

Levi jeans

Wrangler jeans

LEI jeans

Rider jeans

Jeans of shiney metallic blue

Splendously tailored,

meticulously tattooed

Blue-eyed genes, skies are told

Brown-eyed genes, earthly bold

Green-eyed genes, sage of old

Hazel-eyed genes, mixture sold

Tattooed-eyed genes, future's unfold.

"Disciple, you are a turd!"

Huge, big guy, boldly bald,

multi-colored tattoos up and down your arms. So proud to be here, no
shame at all. Tough as nails, tattoos presentably, noticably, couragiously
enthralled. Eat-up with the tattoo faze; tattooed starved, artistically
crazed. Tiny pricking needles puncture your body scene; even though,
the Bible warns, you know what I mean. This day and age, "I don't
care." Into computer, sadistic, electronic warfare.

"Guns are faster than friends"

"tattoed on" the inner flesh of his bicep. God, I LOVE built, muscular arms. Satan I, what AM I going to do with you? I AM THAT I AM means nothing to you. Satan II got dislodged, fired for "dottling on" the Shop-a-Lot #666 sales floor pushing a broom. I was so mad, angry coming so close wrestling with his agnostic spiritual Balrog. He did not believe in God. His reconstructed square jaw from a near fatal car wreck, brown hair and brown eyes – I came so close changing, confirming, "winning on" him to our side. What a waste of time, Kinetic energy, Holier than Thou, spontaneous combustion belief. Lost cause snatched, jerked away from me like a poor, wretched thief.

Satan's II almost disasturously endangered species car crash miraculously recovered life should have showed, convinced him WHO was in charge. Our conversation about good-looking pirate, Johnny Depp, actor, pioneer, martyr of our own validated commonwealth of Egypt, a big lush "turn on." Inheriting $40,000 from brother, Micah, if his death occurred. Wondering if your statement, "yeah, you'll laugh all the way to the bank" is devastatingly true. Unemployment, pixie burgundy locks, endowed live-in, stroking softly your chest hairs putting you to sleep confessionately construed.

Working for the Zion, Egypt jailhouse, prison now – what a great job for you. A better opportunity, career came your way. God, I miss you, tell me you've been saved. Tattoed in my little black book of upcoming saints, my heart prays fervently for your awakening soul mate.

Ms. Mary, USA, kindred wife of sturdy, solid, ruddy Satan I was beat by her ex-husband, ran "around on" and shunned.

"How old were you when you had your first child?"

"15."

"Boy, that's young."

"I was 17 when I got pregnant. 18 when I got an abortion barely old enough to sign the papers. – 10 weeks along. The father of the baby shot himself. Why did you get a divorce?"

"He would beat me and run "around on" me."

"Oh, I had a similar experience, circumstance. Gideon left me for a girl he got pregnant. I flipped out and went to House of Horrors, Wax. I was off my medicine, Lithium. He would show me pictures of his previous fling, lover in bed, drank constantly at the Dove Club, and go out with 5 different women all at one time. Show me your tattoo, please."

"Okay."

Ms. Mary, USA lifts her pants leg up clear to the top part of her thigh. The most beautiful tattoo I have ever seen was revealed.

""Did it hurt?"

"Yeah, I won't lie to you."

Beautiful orange coyfish displayed in azure turquoise blue water was exhibited, presented from her shapely thigh down to her ankle. Satan I and Ms. Mary USA are a perfect couple, item. They are both tattoo literate.

Ms. Mary USA is precisely 5'5" tall guessing to the best of my ability. Her luxurious mahogany straight brown silky shoulder length hair accenuates her doll face and a "mole on" her cheek. Satan I also has a similar "mole on" the back of his burred, barren head. Ms. Mary USA and I have a solemn bond together – both of us being sexually abused and dumped.

"I've been used like a dishrag, and, I don't think I can do it physically with a man anymore," sharing my personal secret. Ms Mary exits, leaves the privacy of the smoker's lounge, break room.

Jeans/genes

Protect your jeans/genes by all means cherish, relish your true blue jeans/genes cold compresses and drug free care mutually-worshipped and stylishly shared wild cat fever and forever denim Break through in the science, fashion millennium

Press them, starch them for the common good

If you ain't got jeans/genes, you wish you would

Carry them around in your back packs makes a good pair of comfortable slacks

Rip them, fade them, take them off

Don't bust the zipper when you cough

Hang them "up on" a honored flag pole salute them, pollute them through the holes

Wrap them around your head in a turbin

Don't forget the scotch and the bourbon

Watch them sigh as they say good-bye out the window, navy genetic dye

The man in the moon wears jeans/genes, too Blue face, blue mood, blue hairdoo

Natural jeans/genes are the most popular best

For they are the ones admired, more or less

Designer jeans/genes for dogs and cats

Incest rabid, rampant for breeds like that

Jean/gene dew rag bandanas in paisley print

Hereditary chromosomes vaguely sent

Red scarves and hats will not do

Everything has to be denim blue

Down through the ages, jeans/genes survive

Is it any wonder, they're still alive?

Generation of tattoos, computer age

Hippies, druggies started the bloomin' craze

The most important question, of course, is "Are you saved?!"

Tattoos, jeans/genes go hand in hand

Throughout the universe, the world, the land

The brand of jeans/genes designates class

Worn, by Catholic teens to mass

Come one, come all – jeans/genes don't care

They're tough, they're rugged, sturdy, and, they wear

Jesus wears jeans "tattooed on" our hearts

God approved, Christian induced ink march

Gypsy's dances, ogres, fairies, blue

Where the hell is your tattoo?

Spread the fever of artistic fame

Tattoos and jeans/genes produce, instill no shame

I wonder if Corinthians, Ms. Mary USA's niece, knows what "is on" my mind, what I AM thinking. Sometimes, I don't give a SH#T; but, I do.

Satan I, Ms. Mary's husband, turns "me on." He says I AM too old for him, and, I AM a jack _____. I can talk about anything to Satan I; especially, sex moves – licking the crack of an _____ and "blowing on" it, sucking toes.

"You have to be a good kisser. It doesn't matter what size you are, as long as you are hard."

Zachariah, Uriah, Zephariah, Satan I are in the _____ing club. _____ this!!! _____ that!!!

Satan I rudely, crudely makes the comment, suggestion that Zephariah's belovéd girlfriend, Ashes, has never given her common law spouse a blow job. That is a must. Zephariah has his initials and the symbol "brotherly love" tattooed on "his skinny, long arm.

Something's gurgling in my car, automobile engine, "Oh, my God!" I can't take anymore, afford any repairs. Having just received my car warranty, "120.00, in the mail again – stupid me, I had lost it, I unexpectedly, accidently give God the middle bird of paradise fly up your nose finger.

Why did I do that? guilt ridden shame over floods me. The gesture reminds me of good-looking Satan I. He would be proud of me; but I AM not, hanging my head in a muddy puddle of shame, remorse.

"It's just the heater warming up," the gas station attendant owner, J.C. consoles, informs.

"Nothing is going to happen, go wrong with that car."

Having driven bombs all my life, this 2005 black Aveo is my precious baby. Thank God!

St. Jude, Jude the dude, is my all-time, favorite assistant manager. I can talk, converse to him and St. James II, the other older assistant manager about anything and they won't reprimand us for cursing, swearing. St. Jude, his bright brown eyes and cute smile – "How exciting!" "Awesome." repeatedly expressed, conveyed filters through my brain waves, mind. I would do anything for him and St. James II; even climb ladders, washing high, tall windows ordered per the hottie young co-manager, Pharoah, Pharisee – Mr. Tempermental. Adelanté. Abierto. Under his control, power. – "on" throned. Set us bondaged slaves free! Let our cry "come on" to Thee.

"Jude, you don't have any tattoos, do you?" His remark, retort uncanny for his sweet, kind disposition:

"You don't know what I have."

"Get me that tomato ketchup poem, story. I definately want to put it in my book. St. Jude, you're our ticket out of here." I don't know why – this thought, reason in my head perplexes, haunts, evades me. Would I be with admired, elated, positive, down to earth, black-haired St. Jude? I don't think so. We are too good of friends, buddies. In college, he confessed, relayed he had red, white, and blue flagged, statue of liberty spiked hair and saw his friend turn into a dinosaur.

"I was messing with something I shouldn't have been messing."

I know what he "was on" – acid or mescaline. St. Jude doesn't seem like the type. He is clean cut, straight forward now. An immediate loving, beautiful brotherly bond went out and my heart fluttered with desired anticipation. St. Jude, patron of pain and suffering, is a sorceror and didn't even know it. He dreamed the customers were coming toward him as blocks of icicles.

"Jude, that is a panic attack."

Sitting in the dark car one winter night because of the 20 feet rule from the dreaded, condemned Shop-a-Lot building, no smoking allowed, the partially abandoned parking lot looms around us like a theatre in Phantom of the Opera.

Zachariah proclaims, professes, "St. Jude has a dick ring, puts it in the freezer. Trinity, his wife, loves it." She is a natural beauty. I AM in shock! I can't believe my ears. How kinky! Jeremiah has a tongue ring. I know what that is for.

"I had a vibrator, and, used to use "it on" my clitoris, pissing in the floor, tried to stick a vacuum cleaner hose up me. I don't do that anymore." (Now, that's horny.)

Aunt Beautiful Patience had given my brother, Micah, & I the green vibrator. The head of the sexual apparatus, contraption stunk where I had stuck it up inside my pussy so many times.

Chloe, Zachariah's live-in women, old lady, smartly remarks, chides: "You need a black man, Mae, white men will treat you like SH#T." (As if, I haven't been treated like SH#T before. I should be used to it.)

"I made a vow, promise to my brown-eyed Grandmother, wonderful strength, not to go out with any black men."

First cousin, Job, had researched our genetic family tree and discovered we possessed, inherited nigger, black blood in us. – the negroe slaves.

Tables are turned.

"Jayden prefers men over women, Mae, he's gay!"

Zachariah concludes the lively personal, private conversation, gossip, shop talk:

"I think Chickie Prickie is a cover up."

"I thought that, too. I wish Jayden would break up with Chickie Prickie. If he ever gets ahold of my pussy, he won't be gay."

The fourth person, counterpart in the old white lumina car, vehicle "sitting on" my left side in the back seat, Trinidad: "I lived behind him, and, I never saw any girls go in and out." St. James II is a Viet Nam veteran, friend, comrad. Nervous – smoking one cigarette after another – "He's ready." "We've got to stop meeting like this, Mae," he funs with a twinkle in his eyes. – one cocked.

"James II tell us some war stories."

Zachariah counteracts this interested request. "He doesn't want to talk about it." The drunken buddy turn-over SH#T house scheme was hilarious, hysterical. How did you work in a sewing factory?

Trying to understand, I didn't want to talk about House of Horrors, Wax either, and, Forgiveness didn't want to talk about prison, half-way house.

One of my best alcoholic, junkie friends, cronies, chums, Forgiveness, was apprehended, thrown into jail, prison for 7 DUI's and counterfeiting $20's. Why she did this crime I do not know because her daughter, Sadducee, had just received a $200,000 inheritance from her blood father, Disobedience.

Sadducee fornicated at 16 years of age conceiving a baby girl child with a grape wine "stain on" her precious pale face. Sadducee conceived a total of 6 kids, 2 born out of wedlock while Forgiveness was incarcerated in prison for 2 years. "On crack," the children were taken away from her. The last child's name was Abigail Lee. Sadducee had given up her life to the Lord, Jesus Christ; Forgiveness, her Mother, wasn't ready. How can you go to prison and not be saved, anyway.

All I know, Forgiveness's dishwater blonde hair and big, wide brown eyes didn't belong there, and, I AM sure her bubbly, exuberant personality didn't fit in either or did it? I can't imagine.

These brave, heroic people are "tattooed on" deep inside the gray matter wrinkles of my compassionate, arrayed soul.

Cauldron, cauldron

Forgive, forgotton

Will you be pardoned?

I don't have tattoos, I have battlescars – exploratory emergency surgery, ruptured, exploded appendix, peritonitis – slit clear down my belly to where the sun don't shine. I don't do needles; likewise, I AM not getting a famous, fad tattoo anytime soon. Apprehendo.

Samaria, her tattoo of understanding LOVE or something like that – I cannot ever remember exactly what the Chinese symbol means – is "inked on" the side of her fleshy neck – ouch!

Samaria's warm round olive eyes gaze into my astonished navy blue genetic dye behind my concerned, wise purple rim glasses, spectacles. Her soft chestnut brown hair lays "peaceably on" her shoulders. Sincerity and admiration are prayfully returned.

"How in the hell can you be with a man physically after being raped and watching your Mother being raped in front of you?"

"I don't know, I just do. I beat a man with a baseball bat off my Mother when I was 8 years old."

"God", I shake my unbelievable head in horrified agony, resentment.

"Don't you ever say that again."

"You've confused him, Mae."

The most gorgeous loveable child I have ever seen looks dearingly up at me sitting comfortably in the Shop-a-Lot cart while I AM people greeting and says, "I love you" the first time I ever met him. Samaria, go forth into the world, be safe, happy and live life more abundantly. You and your darling, awesome son can do no wrong. I AM worried about you – pregnant again and facing bankruptcy.

Saudi Arabia was a girl with short, chopped pink hair. I dyed her hair strawberry with blonde streaks.

"You'll have to pull it through the cap perservations, tiny holes, yourself, I AM afraid I'll hurt you."

"You're pouring a whole can of "chili on" one hot dog!"

"Eat."

Leaning her head over the ceramic bath tub, the whole filled-up clear tub bath water turns reddish-brown. It was surprizingly repulsive, muddy-colored.

Her new abiding apartment door would not lock, and, Saudi Arabia's just founded kitty, Pandora, like Pandora's box, was residing inside by her lonely self worrying anxious Saudi Arabia to death, to no end. What an appropriate name for a cat!

Saudi Arabia dyed her normal-looking hair back pink the very next week. My novice, amateur beautician, hairdresser accomplishment to no avail, shot to hell. Oh, well, I tried. Saudi Arabia's whole entire back was etched, tattooed in unfinished artwork by her father, a tattoo artist. Deranged, crazy-eyed dolls holding chain saws produced, ignited fear in my unbelievable psyche. Why would anyone want tattoos of evil, deranged, psychotic "dolls on" their back?

Saudi Arabia would tell, relay tales of being locked-up in a mental place, sorority house. The white coat nurses would wake her in the middle of the night out of a dead sleep to observe, watch her spit saliva through the pierced hole in her lower lip. She later conceived a boy male child, offspring named Leeton.

Saudi Arabia was taken back, shocked at the personal saga, story of my separated butterfly pussy lips. The black iron railing slicing my vagina in two during my first grade year in school. I was swinging to and "fro on" the sharp porch railings. The doctor called, pronounced the sensitive hanging lips, membranes flabia, tablia or something like that. It was nothing to worry about. I should have had stitches, sutures. The burning was intolerably so bad, I had to pour a glass of cold water in the slit wound when urinating, urination, pissing.

Josiah, a flaming, charming red head, whom I met at Jordan's and Christian's wedding reception "sucked on" the sensual odd dangling fleshy areas producing exotic ecstacy, delight pulling the growths one at a time in his wet mouth. What a "turn on." After making passionate love, pleasurable beyond belief sex at his friend's lake cabin, black stringy diarrhea embarrassingly poured from my anus, butthole while sitting "alone on" the commode.

Estranged, uncomfortable complete silence, endured the entire trip home in his army green sportscar. Josiah was not scared, turned-off by my personal, private abnormality.

Josiah & I met at the wedding reception uniting my previously, impromptued, affaired boyfriend – blonde-haired, light blue eyed Jordan and envied, endowed musically inclined, talented pianist, first wife, Christian.

Slow "dancing on" the loud, crowded ballroom floor, casually talking about the silver fillings in his teeth was a differently exciting, unique conversation coming from this up-coming, future attorney, lawyer, Josiah.

That same very night, Forgiveness, her boyfriend, and myself swiftly kidnapped Galacian's live-in fiancé, Scripture Presbyterian, rushing madly to the King of Hearts secret, trashy hang-out. Galacians was locked-out, forbidden, ostracized from the stark, dangerous dwelling, bar.

"OH, you're one of those good kissers, Mae." Scripture Presbyterian complimented, remarked feeding my flattered, lustful low self-confidence, ego, esteem.

Shoes were tackily taken-off and "placed on" the set-up card tables, and, Forgiveness forgot, left her Mother's, Ms. Judgement's, expensive Calvin Klein raincoat "hanging on" the apparrel rack, pegs in the Zion, Egypt exclusive clubhouse hallway, corridor. Damn!

Another wild episode, experience involving my blood sister, Forgiveness, and coveted Josiah occurred when I looked to the heavenly stars, "God, is this a reverse?" The bright, profound stars tattooing the black nightly sky seemed so far away as I conveniately answered my own questioning, possible troubleshooting. "Knocking on" the law firm's office prominent door, Forgiveness and I let ourselves in interrupting a late night evening, after hours legal meeting, gathering. Use your imagination. The race, creed of tattoo phenomenon. I "AM on" a mission for Jesus Christ!

"Hello."

"Joy, what are you doing?"

"Nothing – making tea."

"Guess what! Greece/Greek came over today visiting over Free Will's house. I'll think I will have an affair with a married man."

"No, Mae, you can't have an affair with a married man."

"You know he's the one who ate my pussy while I "was on" my period. He said it didn't taste that bad. I was 24.

"Oooo. I could have gone all day without hearing that!"

"We were in the bathtub together and everything. That's when I was dating Gideon. He remembered that."

"I asked him if he told Karma, his wife. Greece/Greek said, "I AM not an idiot!" He told the story about seeing this other girl and took "Karma on" his jaunts to the frequented bars. The girl came up to them, "Who's this woman?!" Greece, Greek replied, "that's my wife and if you hurt her I will break your neck!" I wouldn't hurt Karma for the world. 26 years ago, I told Free will, my next door neighbor, that if Greece/Greek comes over again, I would tell the police or tell Karma. Greece/Greek is an Aries – very compatible. According to Jeanne Dixon, St. Peter represents the sign Aries. She had a vision in a Cathedral. Aries is the greatest sign there is because Peter was the first who professed that Jesus was the son of God. St. Jude represents Aquarius, St. Matthew represents Capricorn, and ST. John represents Leo. That is all I know, remember. I don't know who represents Scorpia like you, Joy. I have no idea why all my best girlfriends are Scorpios. This astrological sign represents sex, the loins. Aunt Beautiful Patience, True/Trust/Truth and Forgiveness were all Scorpios. Uncle Humor was kin to Edgar Cayce. He's right up there with Nostsradomus."

"Who's Edgar Cayce?"

"You know he's the one that was the sleeping prophet prescribing curative herbal drugs while he was asleep. He has a hospital in Virginia. Nostradomus said the world was going to end in 2012; but Edgar Cayce said we humans could change the course of the world. That is what this book is for. Edgar Cayce "slept on" his school books and read the Bible 10 times before God finally came to him.

Greece/Greek was over here for 2 hours today. I fixed him hot tea. We read my poems, poetry. He wants to go in it with "me on" the publication. He said, "Get ready." I think he's impotent, but, I don't care. It was so good to see Greek/Greece. We had fun; but, I don't trust a man as far as I can throw them; I only trust God."

"Nooo. Mae, that is adultery."

"I just want to kiss him to see if I can still kiss. Wonder what Free will's Mother, Godspell would think. Godspell is 70 years old and looks 50. She says her beauty secret is good genes. Greece/Greek must have been a surprize messenger from God!"

"No, Mae, we are not going to do that."

"Well, Jayden is committing fornication with Chickie Prickie. That's what he gets. Greece/Greek made a pass at me trying to grab my pussy in mid air without touching me. "Quitt!" It turned "me on." He was a perfect gentleman."

"The spirit is willing but the flesh is weak."

What was I thinking? Lust of the genetic blue eyes, black pupils of old times. I can see. "Wash your eyes in the Holy water and say 3 Hail Mary's." Repent. Why do you go to church for? Greece/Greek read the Bible 4 times. That was his college. Jesus – Man of the year 2009.

God, help me drive this chariot to work. " Who is driving this chariot, Mae?" Me or you." Adam Lot had better be watching this show at store #666 #999. Dad, Perseverance, & Dr. Sweden have a front row seat. Dr. Sweden, psychiatrist, psychoanalysist at OUR LADY OF MERCY, told you were afraid of "sex." I laughed, hee-hawed in his face. I had endulged, engaged in sex at 16. It made him mad, furious. Why didn't I believe him? The description of the Rorschach Ink Blot Test given by the good-looking awesome psychologist must have revealed this result, conception-blood running down Mary's leg. Belovéd DR. Sweden also told, advised you to get out of Mom's, Loyal Dedications house and get a job; but he didn't know how hard it was to find a good-paying job in Zion, Egypt.

Zion, Egypt is not like Nazareth. A good-well-paying job is hard to find; especially in a small town, community; I wanted to go to college. I could not afford to move-out, but, I wish I had listened to Dr. Sweden; maybe, all the horrible, catatrophic fights, brawls, knock down drag-outs would have ceased with Loyal Dedication.

I hope Adam Lot appreciates this!! Lights, cameras, action . . .

The smoking ban, Obama, and McCain for President pisses me off. What is the world coming to? I wanted, voted for Hillary Clinton. She put up with more SH#T from her husband, ex-President, " slick Willie" it's not even funny. I AM higher than a blooming kite-meds-Lamictal, Geodon. I AM white trash; my SH#T stinks. Stay-calm! Calm my ass! All is well! Hell! I have to go to work. Keep your mouth shut. Oh, I have already blown that! "Make my tongue my slave not my master." You don't know who your enemies are at Shop-a-Lot. Good girl, Wrangler. Sleep at "peace on" the couch, and, keep "Tara," the fort down. OCDC. Panic attack. Tattoo my ass! All the ashtrays are out. Out the door. Jesus, you go.

You are the propitiations for our sins. I AM a hypocrite in a den of thieves, anyway. All I know, is you had better not leave my side, groom, forsake me. Selah!

Love ya', bye. Now, what plane are "we on"? All is fair in love and war, satan. I AM not letting Jayden out of my sight. What is in that cistern Holy Water, anyway – olive oil, mineral potent refreshing "everlasting on" $H_2 0$.

The Holy Spirit, GHOST, Comforter

God _____! The Holy Spirit!
Have you ever thought of that?
The devil is so evil, conniving, treacherous
Gracie is overweight, obese, big & fat
Your body is your temple
You mean you've blasphemed silently
The Holy Spirit, Ghost
And you are still alive?
Ms. God and her Husband, God,
Did not make, let you die?!
That shows you how great, something
about the Lord Jesus, anyway
When you accidently rebuke the ghost.
The Holy Spirit is not going anywhere.
He stands firm, unremoved, Almighty,
Heavenly Host.
Now, you know that is a punished,
eternal sin.
You will never be forgiven.
We will seek Jesus's forgiveness
"forever on".
That way we will *always* be living.
Ms. God is superior, over ranking
Over Grace.
Her compassionate, heartfelt love shows
If Gracie ever gets up to Heaven
The father of lies will surely know.
Oh, her name will be in God's

Black "Book of Life".

Gracie can write her name cursively well;

If not, we will abide, sojourn

with her in a coal fed furnace,

Doomed, condemned hell.

Oh, we can witness for the Lord

Jesus Christ down there.

Damnation will not stop our fight.

Against the devil and his evil plans, ways.

Undercover satanists, Christian rights

And knights unite.

Oh, Lord Jehovah, give me a drink

of water.

Pass the glass around to all of us,

PLEASE.

If Gracie Bathsheba dies suddenly

Tomorrow.

We're in big trouble, doo-doo-up to

our eyeballs, shaking, sinning knees.

God Bless the connecting Holy Spirit, Ghost;

New Jerusalem.

That is the way it should *always* be.

Cover your butts you _____ holes!

God knows you didn't mean it.

Diablo, the devil full of hate,

Discord

I hate, can't stand the black

Monster's SH#T

Terminate, cast him out off of

The face of the Earth, living hell

Have "mercy on" us oh, Lord.
Behind enemy's Satan's war lines,
White sorceror, witch army chief
I AM sorry to make you think that;
The devil, Damien has already
Crushed, got me hostige free.
There is one thing I do know:
Oppress, stand up to the devil
And, he will surely flee.
Watch it! Why does God take
our bull SH#T?! I don't know.
God knows exactly what you're
thinking, anyway
When you "put on" a flattering,
Two faced, false pretense, fakey,
God forsaken show.
By God, I know He is forgiving,
Merciful, Loving-Kindness
A hopeful church rebel sinner,
Good Christian I AM not.
I want to feel, see His Face, Nose,
White gloved, gloried Hands.
I would gladly eat His inspirational
snot.
Why does He dump all this devastating,
handicapped "trash on" us?
When you mess with SH#T, you get
"shit on."
Just let me touch your flowing
jean robes – Heal me Jesus;

Heaven I don't deserve to view, go . . .
The light's too bright amazingly so.
Just place me in the suburbs
of Heaven.
This is all I know.
I pray fervently there will be no more
Fiery, disrespectful spiritual wars
Master Christ's slaughtered sword
of Peace until the righteous end
The Anti-Christ, beast of dark angels
Will "turn on" you, stab, rip you
In the back
All I know, devious, corruptive
satan is not your friend.
Your back will heal, you must
"go on" with God's strong force and multiply
To the land of promised honey,
Last futile days
You know Who's gonna win.
Tattoo artists, merchants will come and go
'Till the world is one big upright
Golden Cross
Evil, hate, jealously won't stand
Their ground
Until not one soulful fleeced lamb
Is lost.
When freon air-conditioned hell
Freezes over
The wrath of God knows well
Satanists are human beings, people, too

The sick, wicked, weary world
Won't rest, sweet Jesus
Until we're all saved and come
abide with you.

Battle, War Zone, Devastation

Dear GOD, Jehovah,

Look at all this mother _____

Bull SH#T!!! Zion, Egypt has been hit drastically hard! State emergency 2009 relentless, repulsive ice storm – Armaggadon, left behind, fateful, exasberating alarm. Thank you loving, electrical, reknown bastards for coming, rescuing us unlucky striked peoples aid. Satan has beat us this time in our endless fight. Have faith as a yellow-bellied mustard seed. Hope, Amariah, Joy help, Bless "us on" in our damned plight, flight. Please, don't let one more branch, tree limb fall again: cracking, crushing us "down on" the dark, hard ground. Fires, disaster overwhelms us all, living hell abounds, punished, abandoned, furious, euthanized dog's fatal, deathly pound.

This tattooed rewritten Bible, *Jeans/genes* is behind schedule, due date shot to burning hades, hell. Our yards are in feared shambles, disgrace. Our houses, roofs are condemned, cursed, fearless leader, oh, well.

We still LOVE you, Lord Jesus – about face. Clean-up is dipping in our empty pocket books, purses. We're in our last, end of the world days. I AM not going to the enemies other side no matter what happens, what the scapegoat beast does to me, clenching jaw-tightened teeth. Devout, divine Christians, we all have to pull together in our tearful, hurt feelings agony. Begging, praying for "everlasting on" God forbidden catastrophy, winning promised mercy.

Thank you truthfully for letting me vent, speak my mind sinfully, openly in this test.

"The wages of sin is death."

When will we ever rest?

Tawny "Mae" Harris

Gypsy Sky

(Azul Celeste)

P.S. Forgive us for our hatred, enmity. I know we have disobeyed you and such foremost and "fore on." We are human beings not swatting black, nasty fruit flies. We LOVE, you, anyway. All I know, we deserve this ghastly fire and brimstone. Our lost causes we plead to Thee. Follow the depressed, desolate Eastern star. He is here. We just have to find Him. That is my opinion. Please show us where the true, genuine Jesus lays and stay exactly, unchangeably the way you are. My Jesus is here. "Death to Life" "tattooed on" Jayden's bare arm.

Where was Ms. God through all this devastation? Purity, compassion, consolation heavenly from afar.

Who did I marry, Almighty Ruler, Heavenly Father we trust?

Gold cross protective, miracle, magical ring. One patient day at a time until your frayed nerves, destroyed heart sings. We and God together will get through this mess, amidst all this "destruction on" belovéd, Blesséd Angel wings.

Now, all the virtues will "be" listed here: the ones that don't habitually complain. The Lord, God, sends down His tears, piss, rain-devout showers from "above on" – the undeserving unjust; and, also, justly Earthly arid tundras, dry deserts and torrains.

LOVE is a green-eyed cherub with one brown dot in her eye. She "overdosed on" morphine. I do not know why she had to die.

HOPE is my strict, defiant nurse practicioner. Every blonde straight hair has to "be" in place. She is my caretaker for life.

Professional, kind slips white sewn lace.

CHARITY is so beatiful and so prolific. Her family of 4, 2 twins, 8 grandchildren: 7 boys and 1 precious cleft pallet newborn girl. In debt all our life, we still make amends for sure.

JOY is my best friend now. What would I do without her? Bold, strong-willed, straight forward like a lion, tough circumstances she unfurls.

COMPASSION is a *beautiful*, lovable scarecrow. Old hippy, House of Horrors, Wax inmate. She deserved the best in existence, life. Our close bond will never sever, discenerate.

CHEER makes me laugh all the time. Her awesome soul sister wit and humor pervail. "I AM going to beat you!" At my cash register flaws, mistakes she does joyfully, hillariously yell. A fellow Aquarius-with her presence we will never fail. We'll stand together, stick through high water and hell.

LAUGHTER, my belovéd 2nd stepmother doesn't know what to think. "What AM I thinking?" Let's have a fun before dinner drink.

HUMILITY – I'll never forget her funny, vivacious storytelling, incessant, talkative nature and such. "Yes, Humility, God sees us." I loved her so very much!

HUMOR – my uncle I can't say enough. Helped raise my scrawny-bad, you don't know "jack S#IT ass. Never touched a "hair on" my head, anyway. Our relationship, communion will always last.

WISDOM – unfathomable, irreplaceable Aunt. Uncle Humor's loving, sneezing, loyal wife. God Bless you "forever on." Can't ever say enough about her either. Secret, hidden jewel family stories she told. Turquoise *jean* seas, *gene* fables, tales of old.

TEMPERENCE TRANQUILITY was a nun at OUR LADY OF MERCY. Tutored me in History studies, classes. Cried when I told her I thanked God for my eyes when I "was on" acid.

TRANQUILITY TEMPERANCE was another kind nun dressed in black habit; if, you don't think that was confusing.

Read "Our Town" together – our voices calmly musing, quietly soothing.

_____ you devil, demons and the horse you rode "in on." I just want you to "be" saved. What about the men, women, and children left "behind on" final judgement day?

Fighting evil with evil uniting, combining yoked with unyoked, conglomerating good with good

"What do you think I AM?" Some kind of super, wonder woman, super being, supernatural power, meek official in sheep's clothing, pure Monk's perfect, religious hood?

PEACE: creative of all things Getting up there in years Visible & invisable mysteries shown-seen & unseen – Des parado irotic coincidences occurences. One of the most classiest art teachers alive & family friend I have ever known.

HONESTY: cast the Lord, Jesus Christ in everybody's heart, soul, minds, thoughts, spirits in the land, the world, universe. Balding, brunt, to the point, unrehearsed. Thank God for your birthday, chocolate cake diarrhea rebirth.

THANKFULNESS: never, ever was I so glad to see somebody at OUR LADY OF MERCY!

Pleasant, uplifting – a pearl prized in a abalone oyster shell personally. Glad to have know 'ya, Thankfulness. Stout bloody Mary's, colorful green parrots mimicing _____ you! jam cakes, crocheting, & me.

Rev. Elisabeth's sermon today 1-25-09 "was on" Jonah and the belly of the whale. Moses, Ms. Purity, Soul, Dr. Bethlehem, Jerusalem were there, present. Ms. Righteous, cousin-in-law. Genesis, and, first blood, genetic cousin, Job, were no where to "be" found, seen. Pooh! I sat with a visitor, newcomer in the very back pew of Hebrew Tabernacle.

"Do you want me to move?"

"No, aren't you taking communion?"

"I AM not baptized," he sheepishly replies.

"You need to get baptized, honey."

"Do you like our church?"

"Yeah, the people are warm. I've talked to Moses about getting baptized."

Now, Jonah was supposed to go to this particular city, Ninevah, to warn the people, folks that God was going to destroy it because of their sins. Well, Jonah does just the opposite, runs from the Lord God and goes out to sea. The sailors throw him over the boat, ship and the raging, ferocious, crashing waves suddenly, immediately cease. That's how Jonah got into the belly of the whale before the huge fish spit him "out on" land. This time Jonah goes to the city, and, the townspeople, folks fasted and wore barren sack cloths. God changes His mind and the city lives, is not destroyed. Jonah prances to the top of a hill, mountain, "why don't you just kill me; you made me look like a fool, idiot."

Well, this story, saga reminds me of associates, Jonah and St. Katherine Abigail at Shop-a-Lot, hooking-up love machines.

"He squirts before he does anything."

So. My heart goes out to Jonah. St. Katherine Abigail and Jonah get into this big fight, break-up in the smoker's lounge- _____ you! I AM caught right in the middle of this heated argument. Oh, well. St. Katherine Abigail runs and tells Jayden, asst. manager. Of course tattooed, aloof, play the field Jayden does nothing about it. I don't know what I would have done or whose side I "AM on."

Another incidence with St. Katherine Abigail feeling sorry for herself, poor pitiful pearl engages in the conversation regarding her 4 religiously named girls she gave up custody to her divorced preacher husband. Giving her no mutual grievancy, "you're Blesséd, St. Katherine Abigail. How would you like to "be" screwed over, used by 8 men. I don't want to hear about your detailed graphic affairs with your men, lovers.

That's personal!" ("flopping on" his dick.) Of course, now that I think about it, I AM just as bad, I write my personal, sexual affairs, happenings "down on" paper.

"I admire you, Mae, after all you've been through, and, you can still laugh."

Provoking no sympathy, I loved her for this comment.

"St. Jude, what are we going to do with all these _____ ed-up crazy people?"

I can hear Jayden's imaginery voice calling from far away, "Me or the book."

Adopted, orphaned Jayden, where do your genes come from _____ hole! Get out! We women stick together. My family was raised by strong women. The women wore the pants in the family. I AM the weakling, the runt, and I need you, Jayden "Care" Arthur. Does he really "care"? What plane, level are "we on", anyway. That's my story and I AM sticking to it.

WHERE is the car warranty bill - $120 bucks – reality check. God took care of that. Did I throw, discard it in the garbage, trash? I must have S-T-U-P-I-D "tattooed on" across my forehead. Another day, another dollar. *Where* is all my cash? Obama, our President, help us guide this great nation, country of ours Righteous in all our 10 commandments beliefs

one nation under God – the Trinity Tattoo o' our sacred, honored USA flag the "chief."

God is our gun, our truth, our way our *hope* for years to eternally come Blesséd patron saints do pave the road to *peace*

'till all our united, countries, nations are one.

With all my LOVE,

Gypsy Sky,

(Azul Celeste)

Zion, Egypt

I did not see Mose's belovéd priest's wife, Sarah Israel in church today. She must have been "sitting on" the front row pew dressed in her normal black attire, clothing, pant's suit. "*How* are your daughter's, Light and Path doing?" Light is manic-depressive, also, like me with a grown illigentimate daughter out of wedlock, and grandchildren. Light has a beautiful glow, aura, halo around her peaceful features, face. I heard, hearsay, her sister, Path has had 7 abortions. Path gave birth to a lovechild, and, just got married. They had planned to get married under crossed fishing poles at Zion Egypt park. How silly.' I thought it was a good idea. Job, ex-drug addict lord, hot shot lawyer had a love child, Fornication, who is grown and precious. She gave birth out of wedlock to a baby boy, Understanding. All we need is more illigentimate children in our family. Our genes are all screwed-up. I had high hopes for Fornication – a lawyer, doctor or something. Anyway, Job, and his 2nd wife, Jessica – a Taurus and Aquarius relationship had a volatile, heated discussion and Job would blacken Jessica's eye. His mother, Abundance, did not approve of it.

First cousin, Leah & Holy-Spirit, Ghost gave birth to a beautiful, awesome daughter, Garden of Gethsemane – brown lipstick & all. Garden of Gethsemane bore Pride out of wedlock. She should have had an abortion at 18; but, I AM Glad she did not. Her mother, Leah, did not believe in abortion practices, I did in this circumstance.

Garden of Gethsemane was living with an old black man residing in the capitol of the United States of America. The white, caucasion male framed for her unwanted pregnancy DNA test came back negative. Garden of Gethsemane is happily married now and holds down a well-paying job. Pride is all grown up. It is a honor to be genetically kin to her parents who are in Crusade for Christ.

Now, another 2nd cousin, Faith's oldest daughter, Lover Helper is getting married – a big engagement "rock on" her pretty left ring finger.

My dreamed of boyfriend is cuter than her fiancé.

"When are you getting married, Mae?" her father, Genesis, Real Estate broker inquires.

"I AM next; it's my turn." The immature daughter, Lover Helper – long, luxurious brown locks – don't "be" an alcoholic like the rest of the family – wine bottles low. You're too good of a person. – gift of black V-neck cashmere sweater.

I don't need your purse.

I LOVE you & pray for you, I AM your "Aunt Mae" – seven boyfriends at one time are too many, teacher. This 51 year old maid, undercover nun wants to step down and turn back to her evil ways, fleshy, tactile stimulation, sinful nature with one person. I AM married to Jesus Christ. 5 + 1 = 6 – bad luck number; but the 9 in 2009 is a lucky one or is it disaster. Boy, this is a Peyton Place, soap opera, Harper Valley PTA. *What* is in your tattooed genes; Holy water cistern? There must "be" something in the water. What's the buzz? Tell me what's a happening. God comes first and foremost. "The last will "be" first; the first will "be" last – develop patience. Why do I have to "be" last in everything, anyway?

I AM cloudy cyan blue.

"Proceed on" . . . "march on" . . . Wrangler, my belovéd cat thinks I AM crazy. You are *who* woke me up? Does your conscience bother you? *What* was I thinking? Every _____ night, we go thru this bull S#IT, Lord Jesus Christ – Shop-a-Lot #666. We have not got one second to lose – LOVE & war. I AM a nervous wreck. Smoking is the least of our worries, troubles right now. Drive my chariot, spaceship, please.

Chew, swallow – the pills, meds, pharmecuticals for a lifetime, under doctor's care, surveillance "forever on", hopefully not in Heaven or hell. I can feel my eyes tightening – snake, cat eyes – the tattooes disguise, mask, mark of drug & alcohol abuse, addiction. Beware! hearty souls. Life's a bitch and then you die. I AM in credit card debt up to my eyeballs, _____. There! Are you happy? NO VOID, Jayden.

"My cup runneth over." Wrangler is my life. Stay alert! Time to get a "move on."

God, jump in my S#IT one more time when I first wake-up in the morning, why don't cha. I know, you just wanted me to eat, fill my belly – okay? Don't do that again. I know I AM in an Army but cheez. I don't do mornings. I don't do anything without Wrangler, my belovéd white cat. You made me cry. I AM mad, anyway. All I know, Wrangler had better not die, okay? I will "be" devastated. She's just a cat doesn't compute. TATTOO a cat like branding a cow?

She's mine and she's my baby. I AM so worried about Baptist, Joy's son, I could die. He is too attached to Jeanna, his old black & white fur ball family feline.

What did you do this stuff, drugs for, Mae?

a.) because we can, could

b.) young, stupid & ignorant

c.) fight, bucking the system, establishment

d.) sacrifice for the Viet Nam war. Hippies won the war and we'll do it again. P-E-A-C-E!

e.) peer pressure, conformity – alcohol is a drug.

Drugs, sex, and rock n' roll. Alcohol is a drug, Jayden. "*Why* do we drink? *Why* do we smoke"?

Why do you all do tattoos for? Huh? *What* plane are "we on"? Hold your horses – get off your high horse – stabilize. Do you want to pop pills, do drugs the rest of your life like me? No. I AM wicked; tattooed with grief, remorse, failure. Drugs are EVIL!! Nicotene, alcohol, crack, cocaine, L.S.D. acid, marihuana, pot, heroin, junk, P.C.P. (horse tranquilizer) THC; then there's thorazine, mellaril, methadone, Lithium, stellozine, zyprexa, Geodon. When will this war of drugs ever end? Please. I AM hooked. Hooker in jeans of blue, genes of doom & gloom. Lights, camera, action. I AM having a panic attack. Do you want to do drugs? NO! *Who* are the pushers, God? Drugs of any kind will fry your brain like a sizzling egg in an iron skillet, ruin your entire life, take dominion over your precious soul. Scared – you better "be".

"Calling on" the Angels of Light, white; especially, Michael, Isabella, Gardenia, Elizabeth (naked lady statue), Gabrielle, Francesca, Lavender Rain, Marie. Looking for the out "headlight on" the car, automobile, Jesus! Jesus! I can do it. I can't do it without you, Lord God. "Fight on" against Satan and his evil ways – corruption of our youth. I AM ready to go home. ' Heavenward. Selah!

I can't stand this world, anymore, anyway. God, help me find the Angel key – key to success. "Good girl." Drug abuse sucks! donkey dicks!

I was raised by alcoholics – Uncle Protection & Loyal Dedication. Selah! whatever. Oh well S#IT! He, the Lord, God, Almighty has got you right where he wants you, Mae, as in a chess game, fly in tangled, spun woven Charlottes web, busted anthill. You're busted! Controller of a *mighty*, everlasting universe. Surely, He can take care of your little world, individual important mosaic stone, pebble. Stay alive! Bite the bullet. Take the plunge into the frigid, cold air, weather and go to work witnessing "forever on" for the Lord JESUS CHRIST.

He, God, is whispering softly to me telling me what to do "on matters." I heed, hear His sweet, loving voice. Will I obey every gentle prompting? LOVE, thankfulness, obedience is *how* we show God we love Him. No make-up tonight. "Yes, sir." Please nip these panic attacks in the bud. Thank you. Joy will tell Hope, my nurse practioner about my nervousness getting ready for Shop-a-Lot. I don't want to change medicines. I AM not a guinea pig, pin cushion. You are "getting on" my last nerve, man. I know you and love you. I AM the guru tonight & we're going to do things a little bit differently now. Disobedience – pray, be thankful, not greedy, Mr. Millionaire. God _____ it! I loved you – your spunk, brown eyes & brown hair. Now, put your "shoes on" and walk-out the door. God has perfect timing. Lover of souls: friendship, lover, soul mate, bound in Spirit. I have won Jayden "Care" Arthur fair and square, and, I will surely die because I have seen Jesus's awesome, beautiful face. Automatic pilot – checkmate. I AM pissed – not really. I have to go to work – shoppe of LOVE. Turn off the light. Get your smokes. Say good-bye to the icon Jesus – blind faith overrules discernment.

Thankfulness

Now, flow through me, Lord, Jesus Christ. You are the branches, I AM the vine. My brass doorknob feel completely off the door today.

Please, you can turn my tap water into grape wine.

The unlocked house was still in tact when I came, got home, and, Wrangler was safe, healthy & fine. It's Thanksgiving Day and we all have to work.

No basted turkey & cornbread dressing for me.

In bred *genes* inherited from Moses, Simon Peter, & Paul.

No gathering with loved visiting family. I wasn't called into the Ad office tonight. Kindness was finally back from her extended leave.

No Gracie Bathsheba rolling around in her electric wheelchair spreading intimidating conflict, disharmony.

Lord, Jesus, I thank you for all that I own.

All I've got to say, you are my Man.

Tattooed Khaki jeans & navy *jean* blue shirts may come & go. You've joyously Bless̀ed our Shop-a-Lot clan.

Adam Lot is big, rich, wealthy, & famous you see, smile, greet each individual person hello.

I AM so gratefully *thankful* I have a job.

Now watch store #666 upturn into #999's show.

Green peas, beans, mashed potatoes & such.

Hallelujah! profit sharing, bonuses, stock market will rise.

Thank Jesus, God, Holy Spirit/Ghost, Bless̀ed Trinity for you.

I AM so eternally *thankful.*

I AM alive most of the time.

Gratefulness, unknown, secret, surprized Uncle.

Thank you for all of your inherited $56,000 of lieu, I have mostly spent, almost completely gone through.

Now, I can buy tattooed, embossed *jeans* of *genetic* LEE blue.

I love to "be" cussed, cursed by you, God. I deserve it. "I beg your pardon, you slut." _____ it! Hate me. I AM terrified, and, I AM glad you made me the way I AM. How does He stand me? Don't stand me up, Jesus. We're not tired of your bull. I AM fried – a walking miracle – a "special" fly – swat team. You kept me alive for a reason. I don't mean to "be" disrespectful, disobedient; but, you made me the way I AM – image. You bastard, put me out of my misery, Sir. I LOVE you!!!

Did I leave a cigarette burning? Nasty habit – nicotene is a drug. Don't start! Tattoo art is the drug today passed down from the *genes* of the wierd, strange hippies – flower children. I AM jealous of hard-hearted Hannah's awesome family tree of nieces & nephews "tattoo on" her forearm. She has a D-day, too. Thank God, the butch, is still here, around. I love her! Pat "her on" the ass. Good job! All I know, she is a hardworking bitch, anyway. Hard-hearted Hannah had better not get fired, laid off or we're doomed at Shop-a-Lot #666; #999.

Ecclesiastes, the alcoholic that she is, is getting ready to get canned for missing too many days. *What* will she do – lose her house, *how* will she feed her belovéd pet, dog, miniature Dachshund, move out of state, file bankruptcy. God takes care of drunks, niggers, & little children. "Don't worry."

Dog eat dog world – take care of Thyselves. Pray for her – she's a lesbian, gay and displays several "tattoos on" her feeble, thin frame, body. – gay rights festival. What will we do "Good girl."

The silver chrome water facet keeps dripping cold tap water like a sync chronized ticking clock. It snowed "today on" 3-1-09 – "in like a lion, LEO, out like a lamb - 35° high; low in the 20's. "Good girl."

Wonder if they will change the "Best "Town on" Earth's" name anyway, to Zion, Egypt.

We've got to "go on." without her.

Wonder if tattoos are so crazy, wild in other countries, parts of the world?

The human body is so beautiful – lovemaking sex skins & all. That is the way it should "be." You can't rape a willing soul. "Be" fruitful & multiply is a little bit out of hand – fruit flies. I AM sick & tired of all this trash – God took a dump. I don't believe in condoms, anyway. All I've got to say, pull it out or use the rythm method – dribble, drabble. I hope I can get pregnant – zyprexa makes you sterile. Birth control pills make me want to die with my chemical imbalance in my brain, anyway. I AM 51, and, losing a winning battle. LIFE is a spiritual battle zone. More power in numbers – Catholics have large families.

Where do your *jeans/genes* come from? a clothing, grocery store? Do you know? from a sperm bank? Our tattoos from our *generation* are our scars – battlewounds & we're proud to "be" here like the wounds in Jesus's side, head crown of precious, sticky briars, pierced nails in his Holy feet & "hands on" Calvary that deep, dark day 2000 years ago. *How* could a Father, mother _____ let His son go through that – sad. *Why* did He have to die that way refusing the Angel's hands – our salvation. We owe Him our sacrificial life for a lifetime. How pitiful can you get? Are His shoulders big enough to handle all the burdens, sins, corruption of the world? Yes, And, He can handle, muster your problems, too – all of them. Come, cum to Jesus; He is the only way. Now, I have stooped about as low as I can go to get you "saved."

Look at all those tattoos of the world – they are permanent, irrerasable ink. I want to tattoo my bare chest if I have breast cancer with a colorful collage of my belovéd animals, Wrangler & Lee, a coyfish, and a hummingbird if both scarred boobs are removed, chopped off. Breast cancer runs in my family – the pink ribbon, symbol of courageous chemotherapy, radiation, remission. Jesus Christ has tattooed my heart soul with LOVE, understanding, forgiveness.

Jesus has adopted me for LIFE, I hope & pray, surely "forever on" I will search for Him – my lover. Tramp for the Lord, Jesus Christ. His *genes* will never die from this day forth. I AM an *undercover* nun, satanist, sorceress, white witch, bride of the LORD, Jesus, and, I want to keep my candle burning bright, my oil lamp filled to the brim waiting, watching for His return. I can hear Jayden's imaginary voice calling from the upstairs bedroom: "Come to bed. it's 5 o'clock in the morning. Jack me off."

As I brush my shoulder length blondish brown hair looking into the glass mirror – "Do I look okay, alright, Jesus?" My naked, bare, untattooed exposed Garden of Eden body is yours. I want to grow my hair out long, luxurious like the coveted, speaker of tongues, admired Pentecostals to wipe your humble, elite feet one glorious day, if you will, would have me. An affair with a married man – Greece/Greek? What would Karma his wife say, think? Adultery? Don't tempt, test me. I AM weak.

Satan I, name changed to Ezekial, strength from God, because he is too good to "be" Satan I – good father, morals, doesn't believe in fornication. If Ms. Mary USA & Ezekial broke up, would I hustle him, have a chance. "You're too old for me, Mae." If I married Ezekial, I would "be" doing him a favor. If a Christian marries a non-Christian, they will both go to Heaven according to the scriptures. What was I thinkin? Thou shalt not . . I thought about it.

Fornication, control your stuff with white chili, Free Will, my onry next door neighbor. He fixed the door knob for trade – me. What would his Mother, Godspell think – nothing? She would "be" a great, lovable mother-in-law. I've got to get some. Is Jayden practicing? Will he marry Chickie Prickie? Is Free Will *using* me to get his rocks off? He has been celebant for 2 years plus and he is horny. I AM using him, too.

It feels good to "be" sexually alive after sex once in 15 years – cobwebs. My libidos back after the Lithium withdrawal. Has my hymen, cherry grown back? I desparately want to turn into a whore, slut again. White chili & I would "be" doing each other a favor. "What are friends for?" I can handle it; but, I can't. Is God giving me a man I

AM not particularly totally, wholeheartedly fond of to go to bed with for Christmas? *What* a present! Wrapped up in a bow.

I sincerely, snottily want Jayden "Care" Arthur to "be" my man, love boats secret heart strings attached, "rosined on" a crying, weeping violin orchestra. Will I hold out? I AM married to Jesus Christ – my gold cross banded ring proves, establishes it. Will I break our vow? This would "be" a big step down for me. I "have on" black nylon panties, briefs. Oh my God, this moment of lust is right after attending church services.

Free Will "had on" *jean* blue speedos, bikinis underwear, garments. "I'll show you mine if you show me yours." We did nothing of the sort. Oh God, here we go. We kissed, bird pecked; if, he had french kissed me I might have given him some. Gently caressing the smooth head of his penis, Free Will aroused my pussy stimulating, rubbing it with his warm hand.

"That feels good." I had my casual black Sunday "pants on."

"AM I an ogre?"

"You're good – looking, Free Will."

"So are you, Mae. You've got a pretty pussy."

"I think it's ugly. It has 2 "growths on" each side of it. What will your Mother, Godspell think?"

"I AM 51 years old, and, she'll probably not think a thing."

"There's nothing wrong with your equipment, Free Will," even though the trunk was shorter than I imagined, thought it would "be" after Greece/Greek said, informed confidentially, in private, "Free Will's dick is long & slender & he knows how to use it."

"I love the head of your cock."

The penis appeared to "be" gray, knotty as he jacked-off in front of me turning "me on." I spread my legs wide apart sitting in the sky blue plush velvet living room chair separating my lips of my vagina with my fingers. I was used to rock hard, huge dicks, balls, scrotum like St. Peter Eater's. The tested curse turquoise Chinese rug hauntedly, guiltily lies "unrespectfully on" my in-shock mind, psyche. What happened in this room?

God gave you a good man who takes care of his Mother travelling home every weekend to "be", "check on" her, and, you didn't want him. My long, slender arms drape around his thick neck, "I've got to get back to my job in Nazareth, Egypt."

I so wanted to tell Joy this unexpected encounter with the opposite sex; she was not at home and probably didn't, wouldn't want to hear it, anyway. Will I keep my big, excited mouth shut, closed around brotherly love, agapi Jeremiah, Malachi & the guys as we bull SH#T around the iron picnic table in "The Ghetto," the discriminating outdoor smoking area. Free Will's heavy, shakey breathing slightly turned me off & aroused penetrating sympathy, compassion all at the same time like the slobbering newlyweds, Loretta Lynn, Sissy Spacek in *Coal Miner's Daughter.*

Will I "be" punished? I don't give a rat's _____; but, I do. You paid Free Will back for fixing, repairing the brass door knob in trade. He copped a full.

"Touch it!"

"Don't hurt me, Free Will –

"be" easy." That was a close one.

Just think about the veneral diseases – Herpes, Gonorrhea, syphillis, Aides. You don't know where he's been. Wrap it! "No." I've been dated, raped, and men don't fill a satisfying thing. So, there, "be" it lust.

Humility: you were so extremely joyiously funny, a character. Our trip to Deuteronomy, Egypt was a hit, smash.

What would we do without your good sense of humor? storyteller. Wrapped-up in West Nazareth's bar, poolroom bash?

Perseverence: why did you have to leave us? Divorce the hidden, vacant mark. Tattoo the empty longing fatherly love, abandoned Micah & I needed from your unopened heart.

Kindness: your name fits you so perfectly well. You would think you were 2-faced; but, you're not. Your kind strength & fluent, coniferous attitude. Your loving family comes front center & first.

As CSM, we could not do without you – you're irreplaceable, after God's good graces you do thirst.

Wonderful Strength: Mammy, you know what I thought of you. Idolized, worshipped the ground you "walked on," seamstress. You sewed all my clothes night and day, "sew on." I was only 13 when you abruptly died, passed away from colon cancer. If you had lived, I would have taken good care of you, all disastrous, demonic drugs shunned.

Loyal Dedication: Mom, I don't know how you did it.

Two bratty kids running wild. Alcoholic diseased, brow beatened failures, come now.

If I could have sat down & talked to you, I might now have Lazarus's tattooed, multi-talented love child. The neonates, Alison Rain, Joshua (to kill) Alex had no chance in hell. Acid trips Lazarus & I would have unknowingly dropped. Wanted to pursue a career in college. His fateful suicide death I could have stopped. I will never ever forgive myself for the abortion – a black widow spider I AM poisonly not.

Beautiful Patience: In this world, you have to "be" too kind in order to "be" kind enough. I AM so sorry I drank, so young, your bacardi rum, vodka booze.

That's the only time you reprimanded me. God, I'll *always love you!*

Faith: you were an accomplice to murder. Abortion – that's a horrible relentless fact.

I was hungry, you sent me away empty to the food bank, breast cancer, your dying Pisces ending fate.

True, Truth, Trust: God, True I miss you so much. Aaron, your sexy, crazy husband is still alive by the hardest – his constant horny "hard on" I will truely away from loyally dive. I AM mad, sorry you had to leave. You are my best friend "forever on" Death parted, separated you from me.

Happiness: you are a hoot! You'll liven up the show!

I could do a beautiful "makeover on" you. Toothless wonder, teeth, false, fingernails, dress of yellow gold.

Forgiveness: Ms. Judgement's daughter. Your pretty, awesome face, blonde hair, brown eyes will shine. Went to prison for 2 years – counterfeiting $20's, 7 DUI's. Blood sister, your crime I do not mind.

Praise: country & hard worker beyond belief – a raise/full-time she should have. An ant worth her weight in gold. Shop-a-Lot needs your loyal assistance. You put your personal "problems on" hold.

Ms. Righteousness: you are an admiral, belovéd religious churchgoer. You saved my li fe pumping my stomach when I "o'd on" valium pills. You may think I don't remember that. My gratitude "tattooed on" my heartstrings instills.

Obedience: your fatal car wreck running a stop sign crushed, killed my soul. Christian baby sitter, wholesome, popular 16 year old girl.

I wish you were still alive today. Your distraught, mother, Manna II, your brown hair she could lovingly curl.

Ms. Purity: you weave to & fro with the Holy Spirit in Church pews. I AM jealous of the living, spiritual fact.

Your volunteer work at the Door of Hope.

I would give my eye teeth for a job, career like that!

Cheer: a soul sister, soul mate, good friend – one *who* sticks by me to the end. Age of aquarius – Valentine's birthday. We mutually love to romp & play.

Appreciation: a rich "uncle on" my mother's side of the *genetic* family we didn't know we had. $750,000 - $56,000 spread between 8 cousins.

Thank God for Discernment, divorced grandfather, estranged Dad. Beard, cabin, only son, inherited windfall lieu. Thank God, he birthed you.

Reverent/Respect: the youngest boy of the Aziah clan.

You are the purpose driven.

Thanks for praising my humble artwork. I wish your Mother, Maebelle, was still living.

For you, God has a special "plan on" the meek Earth and in Heaven.

Blesséd: tattoos are proudly bestowed: butterfly, heart with note, star with note, rose, 2 crosses & tiger cub. Please, Blesséd, don't get pregnant; your R's you cannot roll.

Don't "pass on" your *genes* anytime soon. In promiscuous, know it all, eager bearer *loving jeans* behold, unfold. I LOVE *you* more than you'll *ever* know!!!

Titus: has a briar "band on" his arm. He asked if he's in the book. I can find a special place for him. Pages turn, I "hang on" his humor & fondly, searchingly look.

Now, TATTOO is another matter. Smart, technical school to "move on." Shop-a-Lot held him back. Bright future in his stars are won.

Jayden "Care" Arthur (Does he really care?) He fixed the "abrasion on" the top of my injured head. Jayden has a "tattoo on" his forearm dispicting the words LIFE TO DEATH. Is he my Jesus in the flesh? Will the real Jesus, please, stand up? Jesus was not a Capricorn; He was a Taurus. It's a little farfetched that in the middle of the winter pregnant Mary heavy with child & Joseph would "be" turned away from the Inn – how cruel can you get. In the Holy modest manger with barn animals that starry night, Jesus humbly was born into this world to die. I believe that Jesus was born in May, my opinion "tattooed on" the Heavenly sky. Now, what plane are "we on"? That's life forevermore, "forever on."

With all my *faith,*

Tawny "Mae" Harris

P.S. Did Jesus & Mary Magdeline make love – a perfect love?

He was a man in human, mortal form. Did they produce a child? together?

Scotland yard, your life
Taking Mary as your wife
Jesus in the flesh appears
Baptism erases all fears
Christening is the seed sown
Briars crown, nails, Angels flown
Cup of Holy blood, manna bread
His closest followers did they feed
"Fishes on" banks, tattooed walls

"Walking on" water, He never falls
Hold you in the hands of God
From thence you, Scotland, will
forever trod
Paths of light will guide your way
God Bless "you on" this special day!

I AM not through with *Blesséd* search. All I ask, is for her spiritual rebirth. She is not a bloody – *bossy* know-it-all. From God's bosom she will never fall. I can learn a lot from *Blesséd*, anyway. Sex moves, special touch, girl of tattoo *jean* blue day.

What a good wife would she "be". All I ask, is let me urinate, pee. 23% left of my kidneys, don't you see. "Cuts on" her controversive arm, together we fondly bond.

I love her much, charm, contrite magical wand.

Gracie's contradictive audacity better let *Blesséd* go. – attitude sold.

Stories, issues, wonder, self-confidence sublimely untold, blank pages unfold. I can't do without my *Blesséd* love. God is watching over us from up above.

Sometimes, my grated nerves are a little shot.

God, I wish I had never started blasted, dreaded drugs, pot.

"You don't know where I've been," I can hear her say.

"You don't know *how* crazy I AM," yesterday or today.

All our past dues will have to "be" repaid trogan mend.

Our kindred spirit friendship, *genes* will never end.

Hurry up & wait. Now, *what* plane are "we on." If you can't say somethin' nice, don't say anything at all. Yeah, right. Hope for the best; expect the worst. Hope flourises; doubt flees. Leave well enough ALONE. Give me a minute, please. Think positive things; positive things will come to you. Think negative things; negative things will come to you. Good ole' qualms. Reach out your hand, please, to the white Angels.

Help me write this check. Oh, well. I really don't give a SH#T today – Sunday – 3-22-09. Do with me what you want. Welcome to the real world – sinners – evil ways. Overcometh mountains of evil; mountains of difficulty. Left behind – mad, angry, hurt. – The Rapture. I AM in a bad mood. *Who* pissed in your post toasties? Sélah! God – it, Wrangler, puke another hairball. Lead, follow, or get out of the way. You are going to trip me – freight train coming through. Another one bites the dust, ashes. Oh, my God! Pontious Pilate has prostrate cancer.

I am not ready for sex or AM Is? I AM THE SOURCE of everything, Mary Magdeline.

THE SOURCE of hearts so true

You are the conception of *genes*

Relinguished, released in *jeans* of blue. Where is *your* tattoo, pussy willow? All men are full of bull SH#T, crap, anyway; except One, Jesus. The water facet is dripping. It's cold outside & lonely in here; but, you are never ALONE. The furnace is running constantly. God, I wish Benjamin, the Zion, Egypt Heating & air man were here. I feel safe with him proposed to the lovable guy. "Write this book first, Mae, then we'll "be" rich. You know my wife, Argentina, is good for something." I really don't care what she thinks. She was married to my cousin – in-law and she tried to teach me how to drive drinking cherry vodka and sprite. Benjamin took Argentina away from my cousin-in-law, Germany; I think we might "be" kin, anyway. All I know is that I

106

LOVE Benjamin. I AM scared to death by myself – winter moving – in furiously, harsely & mean with vigor of icy fingers of wrath.

I wish St. Jude, assistant manager was "still on" third shift. I can talk about my personal past problems to St. Jude and James II. Fluffy Jethro, dumber than a box of rocks, just doesn't get it after coldly, unemotionally giving me a D-day, dooms day, for calling Gracie Bathsheba a bitch behind her back. "Cauldron, cauldron. forgive, forgotten. Will you "be" pardoned?" My D-day is not up till August, 2009. Adam Lot, deceased, had better do something about these procedures, rules – freedom of speech.

I AM "high on", proud, pleased with St. Jude & St. James II. Pride bars the way, I LOVE how St. James II crosses his legs while smoking one cigarette after another.

I bequeath, give my home, house, Tara, upon my death bed to my belovéd Church, Hebrew Tabernacle. The life insurance goes to my belovéd brother, Micah. No viewing; no memorial services – my body goes to science. St. Mae – my epitaph & a stone, concrete Angel my headstone above my designated gravesite.

My belovéd cat, Wrangler, goes to Godspell or Joy. The book of *Jeans/genes* and all proceeds go to Joy. The black Aveo car goes to Joy's son, Methodist.

All my precious rings go to Abana, Garden of Gethsemane, Lover Helper, omnipotence, Tess Respectance, and, the rest of my belongings the second cousins can fight over. If these wishes are not carried-out to the tee, I will haunt you.

If married, all belongings, house, Tara, and property will go to my husband & children: Mae Psalm, Scott Alex, Jesse Lee, Jody Lee, Seláh Jo, Bond Conner or Christopher Scott, Scott Taylor Conner, Brennan Scott, or Fawn Christiana, Tawny Mae, & Shawn Marie. Mae Psalm will "be" called "song" by her friends and Jody Lee – "Jazz." *Who* did

I marry? *Where* is the husband, Father? Christopher Scott will "be" called "scotch." I hope he doesn't drink it.

It's going to "be" a sad day in hell when I die. Coffee's ready. Ding! I AM not scared to death of dying; I AM just scared of dying. I AM not scared to death of living; I AM jus scared of living. I need a man, one I want to take care of me. I'll rub your back if you'll rub mine. I hope co-manager, King of the Jews is outside at the smoking area – The Ghetto – braving the freezing air, weather after being ex-communicated from the warmth, solitude of the inside smoker's lounge discrimination bull SH#T! I AM choking by myself. Can anybody hear me? Jesus can. Now, young Pharoah, co-manager, is another thing making me climb that tall, forebodding ladder washing top windows. I feel fairly safe, comfortable, edgy with prestiged King of the Jews. Don't want to talk about it, man. It's a honor to know you. Silence is golden. "Thanks for the light." What are we going to do about these cigarette and gas prices, God? I've been smoking since I was 14. You don't want to "be" around me if I quit cold turkey. What a *bitch*!

We are a bunch of unhappy campers! Health reasons. Joseph Abraham, please, don't beckon, frequent my door, belovéd plumber, because of frozen, broken pipes. Now, *who* are you "calling on." Angels, anybody I can get my "hands on" – Jesus.

Jeremiah's here tonight. Thank God! What _____ day is it?

Stay calm. My hands are clammy with sweat. I hate that. – Shop-a-Lot – this God forsaken place. I don't want to touch the customer's hands, crossing them with dirty, filthy currency, gypsy silver. Wrangler, you're eating me out of house and home – cat food. Battin down the hatch – "Tara." Stay calm at all costs. Calm SH#T! Now, God, help me put this "make-up on." I AM very manic-depressive-crazy check – Huh! Life's a bitch then you die. Peace in the Middle East. Faith, fairy dust – sprinkle, sprinkle bitch! You owe me! That's your job. "Oh, God, our help in ages past, our hope for years to come." This particular, special suicide flight is for King of the Jews. Can I trust them? WHO can you trust?

Kindness, CSM, will "be" "there on" this flight, show. "Hang on" to her for dear life. Her oldest son, Mannesah is going to war, battle in Iraq. I AM done praying for you. Now, pray for yourselves. Take care of Thyselves. It's a dog eat dog world out there. I AM prayed out – "prey on." Man of sorrows; acquainted with grief. Fear causes depression. Fight depression like a plaque. Think happy thoughts like when you & St. Paul were in love. Why did God take him away from me? Aides? Dead or alive? That's the last one - #8. Just tell me if he's clean – needles.

"You have fucked up for the last time – time clock." Outburst, out of order. Attention'! per God, Jehovah. "I want this book written!" Where did I go wrong – in life – drugs, medicine.

"Okay," sergeant.

"Keep that mouth shut!"

"Surely to God I can do this, that."

"You are not indispensable, replaceable."

"Now, read Tim LaHaye, Jerry Jenkins "LEFT BEHIND" and get it over with. I have spoken.

"Right away, sir. Damn it!"

"Put your weary head to rest.

Don't you cry no more. The truth will set you free." "Bull SH#T."

I was ever so thankful for a glass of fresh, clean water in hades, hell Zion, Egypt. Same ole' SH#T or is it? A closer, familiar walk with your Majesty. You will not come between me and my God, and I mean You! All of you "be" quiet. Voices divine "be" still. I'll never make it through another Good Friday, Easter – Oh, yes, you will – *cross* your fingers. Thunder, Theology – manic – expressive, possessive, impressive. Spread the Holy "word on" love currents, flowing around the world, universe. Now, *what* plane as "we on?" Variety is the spice of life; "walking on" eggs.

Cut through all this crap, red tape! That was the purpose, attitude of Jesus Himself to save sinners. He was willing, living to "take on" the sufferings, sacrifices of the world, humanity, a martyr of all times; so, we could live life more abundantly – cup overflowing. The punished, slaughtered, beaten, crucified Prince of Peace. The elite sword of blazing fire is nigh in the twinkling blue jean sky. "Here I AM."

I AM so lucky to "be" alive I could die. L-I-F-E – Live – In – Forever – Eternity.

1-God	6-Devil, Satan
2-Jesus	7-Lucky
3-Holy Spirit, Ghost	8-Learning, Growth
4-White Angels	9-Lucky or Disaster
5-Mae	10-Covet

Geneological, Ancestor family tree:

Wonderful strength & Discernment
begat
Abundance, Beautiful Patience,
Wisdom, & Loyal Dedication
Discernment & Garnet?
begat
Appreciation
Hezekiah & Abundance
begat
Faith, Job, Leah, & Rebekka
Beautiful Patience & Saudi Arabia
begat no children (2 abortions – *why?*)
Beautiful Patience & Protection
began no children
Wisdom & Humor
began Czekoslavia & Siberia
Loyal Dedication, Perseverence
begat
Mae & Micah
Faith & Genesis
begat
Samson, Leviticus, Lover Helper,
& Omnipotence
Job & Apple (forbidden fruit)
begat
Sodom & Gomorrha
Job & Jessica
begat

Fornication & Topaz

Holy Spirit, Ghost & Leah

begat

Jacob & Garden of Gethsemane

Rebekka, Gilead

begat

Abana, Luke II, & Tess Respectance

Czekoslavia & Poland

began no children

Siberia & Religious (giggles)

begat no children

Siberia & Shiloh (sperm swimmer)

begat

Holland & Netherland

Samson & Puerto Rica

begat no children

Samson & Deliah

begat

Nathaniel & Jew

Abana began no children

Fornication

began understanding

Garden of Gethsemane

begat Godsend

Leviticus & Ireland

begat

Michael (there is *only* one

Michael & that is the

Archangel, patron of cops,

policeman that saved my

life from an overdose

of pills, medicine), Hallelujah!!!

Sodom & Christmas Carol

begat

Nineveh, Ham, Gratefulness,

Zebedee, & Christian

Gomorrah began no children

Jacob & Noel

began Rachael

Lover Helper began no children

omnipotence begat no children

Micah (beautiful, funny, loveable gay, queer, faggot) began no
children

Mae (single spinster, old maid)

began no children yet – 51 years old & cursed barren o chicken feces
in peaches – witchcraft – mean).

Perseverence & Pearl

began no children

Perseverence & Laughter

began no children

Powerful Might & Ruby Red

begat

Australia, Perseverence,

& Church (flattery).

Australia & Diamond

begat

Esther (bitch – wrote letter knocking me out of St. Genieve college of
my choice) &

Emerald

Church & Opal

began Crucifixion
Esther & Resurrection
began
Cherub & Joshua
Laughter & Mystery (mysterious ways)
begat
Kris Kringle, surity Bagdad
& Promise
Promise & Moscow
begat
Norway (Norwegian), Nun
(fighting, wrestling with the Holy Spirit) & Theresa,
Thessolonians
Ascension began Viet Nam
Viet Nam & Argentina
begat no children
Viet Nam Deborah
begat
Finland (Boo!) &
Amethyst
Religious & Columbia (unknown seen & unseen) begat no children –
    just dogs, canines.

Christmas Carol

Dear Santa Claus (Kris Kringle),

Bah! Humbug! Are the elves all _____ing themselves? Oh my God, what happened today. I picked-up a cold stranger walking in the wicked, cruel artic blast, frigid hay where he could have frozeningly laid, a stray. I have a brand new 2005 black panther areo – the stranded stranger's transmission is out. Please, no suicides this bloody icy year from the rooftops I cryingly pout, desparately shout.

Don't eat yellow pissy snow and don't look for an easy way out. Keep your water facets dripping, the weather, wind outside is frightening. He has put Mother Earth, nature asleep, dorment, solid silenced whitening. Wrangler is cooped-up, den cabin fever; but, it's better than being hit, struck by archaic April lightening. The curse is lifted. Oh, my God, Wrangler is so mystically, awesomely gifted. A – absolutely w – wonderful E – egotistical S – super, stupendous spell bounding o – omnipotent m – marvelous, mesmerizing E – eternally, just like God, Jehovah up listed, majestic purple mountains shifted.

Watch over this bewitching white cat for me, please. We're up SH#T creek without a paddle without her, don't you see. Oh, I AM so sorry I thought, Santa, you were an imbecile. No, I AM the dreaded, troubled twisted imbecile for truth. Prancer, Dancer, Vixen, & Rudolph can tap "dance on" some other poor soul's roof. I donot deserve to "be" here, eat the spared, saved, sparse crumbs underneath your Last Supper's table. I have heat, toilet paper, gas, food, water, and, there are people without a black kettle pot to piss in, and, cronically, disastrously disabled.

It's a terribly hard life to life; but, it gives back what you respectfully, tithely give. I know you are angry, unhappy, mad with us. Gypsy sky (Azul Celeste) is dismayed, disgruntled, cursed, cussed. I want a boy, male baby Jesus, take us Heavenly Easterly star home or bust. Wrapped in humble, tattooed swaddling clothes, I have been Blessed entirely way too much. Hobnobbing with the wealthy, rich folks: silver spoons in their mouth, naughty glass houses, lush, plush presents, fast sporty vehicles, computer game electronic archives and such.

The rich He sent empty away, and, the scriptures, Christmas carols, peaceful Gospel, parables He instilled in us rightly and just. Your barn-shack manger needs to "be" an expensive condo, kingly castle – a shrinely mansion we revertly, religiously cannot touch. Santa's red crimson sleigh had better visit the ones that do without. Down the roasted chestnut chimney with his fungus nutcracker ballet balls, ornaments, "hard on" stuck and can't get out.

Oh, "up on" the roof tops, Ho! Ho! Ho!, anyway. There might "be" a SH#T face drunk, potential DUI victim driving St. Nick's jolly sleigh. An abundant fruit basket from Africa Ensemble "arrived on" my back concrete porch. I did not deserve this beautiful kind gesture, honor, invite to their loving, giving Church, lit torch. This is the first Christmas without cousin Faith alive. Have faith as an abundant, growing mustard seed. Please, keep the needy, bestowed whole hungry world spiritually fed in God abide.

The three wisemen paid their gold, frank incense, & myrrh glorious, respectful, reciprocal tithes. I write this feeble letter, saga, gift toy soldier story by candlelight of ka leid oscope red, white, and, green stained glass. All I know is, Santa Claus has jingle bells "tattooed on" his cracked, bare, fat ass. May the good will, charity family traditions go down "forever on" through the aged generations, and may the book of *Jeans/genes* be a smashing box office hit, and receive a royal, standing ovation.

"Bless on" . . .

yours very *cheerily,*

Tawny "Mae" Harris

P.S. There will "be" no black sabbath Christmas for me in this white winter wonderland. I know where *all* the Blessings flow from in our United States free-loving hand. Happy Birthday, Merry Christmas, sweet Jesus!! I AM so sorry You had to "be" born to die for us. You are the reason, the season, the way, the light, the truth.

The Inn had no room for your, visable miracle birth. Unite all nations together as one in Christmas spirit, lions and lambs peacefully aloof. Shepherd Joseph and Virgin Mary's Bethlehem savior's everliving on" son's loving proof.

"Peace on" Earth, good will towards men. God, *why* do I have to always sin? Home for the holidays. Will I get paid for writing all this bull SH#T? I AM a _____ hypocrite! Will Mrs. Santa Claus get laid, a hicky on her neck, in between her tit?

Poinsettias, red berry holly wreaths flow. French kissing Jesus under the mistletoe. The grimly, nasty Grinch finally saw the light. Merry Christmas, Happy Holidays to *all*, and, to *all* a good night!

Just Jesus & Me

I AM with you 369 days of the year. Hold me, LOVE me 8 days a week. So children, don't worry, be of good cheer. I have overcomed the world – never fear. I LOVE your artistic, creative blue *jean* seas, oceans, rich, rust, brown Earth. Thank you, gracious & everliving God For your electric, miracle happening birth. Right now, it's just Jesus & me. It'll, we'll "be" alright Charity, Kindness; Just wait & you will see.

Genes go down in mandate medical history. _____ you, devil! And, the horse you rode "in on."

Praise the Lord, Jesus Christ! Amen.

Don't break the chain ever again!

Suicide is not meant for women & men alike; it is a crucial sin.

NO, God is *not* a mother _____ ogre. Let me make that perfectly clear. He is the whole world to me. Inbred, cloned, clashed kin, almighty deared.

God is a great, wonderful Father-in-law.

As a bride of the Lord Jesus, white sorceror, witch, just call Him Dad, Paw you all.

I AM awake now. Stay alert! fire & brimstone, tattooed blank jailhouses, brick mortared walls that moan & groan. My wine bottles low, lanterns oil lit full.

Believe me, Holy Christian religion is no bull.

I've dangerously _____ up in my lifetime.

Man, have I been an undercover nun, satanist fool.

War! you mother _____ incest demons! And, yes, your ass is grass!

The real, true Jesus Christ will come again, anyway.

His forgiveness will "forever on" last. One tea leaf left, the Golden

Child. "Hanging on" by a single red thread. Kissed Jesus in the flesh, Jayden's white, honky ass.

Why don't you give him some head? "Sucking on" a chili dog

Prayfully, hopefully he'll forever "be" mine.

All I know is, just give him some precious, spacious time. Wrangler, my haloed white, gold-eyed bewitching cat, feline, furry friend are left mysteriously mystically alone to "be."

His Heavenly Majesty, Sacrificial Lamb, Master of all,

Right now, it's just Jesus & me. I AM so tired of looking, searching for SH#T.

Does this mean I AM tired of looking for You?

I don't want to give up futile, awaiting hope.

I'll find You if it hairlips the forlorn, exalted Roman Catholic Pope. Blinded by faith, I cannot physically see.

Just want to *touch* your healing velvet robes.

Wash, wipe your feet with my long wavy hair meticulously, obviously combed.

Right now, it's just Jesus & me.

If I stumble, slip, fall, fail, I vow "down on" reverent bended knee.

Wanting to witness for you in hell no cold, ice water, just your loving blood stained creed. Right now, it's just Jesus & me.

Special Thanks To:

Jeremiah – his priceless, profound, beautiful, philosophical nature, demeanor, countenance that cannot "be" captured, "grasped on" paper.

Joy – my belovéd best girlfriend who committed, locked me up in shut down insanitarium, mental hospital at Jebosite Haven for my own good, welfare.

Satan I whose name I changed to *Ezekiel*, strength of God, because this young man is too good to "be" called *Satan I*. – loving husband to *Ms. Mary USA*. Hold hands; kiss & make-up; protective step father to her 2 children; giving-up birth rights of his fraternal son for the child's sake – out of wedlock baby; has morals – does not BELIEVE in fornication. Is Church, religion such a forbidden, abominable thing?

"Jesus was just a man"

"You don't know *how* big God's dick is!"

"I AM that I AM means nothing to me."

His "tattoo on" his inner arm, biceps, "guns are faster than friends" whatever that means.

This rebel soul never gave "up on" me & definately is my biggest fan in wanting to read my book writing, journal, *Jeans/genes*.

Gabriel & Dan's persistant, dependable prayers (churchy people) curbing my cursing, "swearing on" the Good Book, the *Bible*. "Mae!"

"I dropped the damn *Bible* in the floor?!" Why did that slip out? I did not mean it! I hated my ashamed, hurt self for the crass, blasphemied exclamation, uncalled for remark. This inseparrtable, love bird couple have a smoking addiction, too, but; alcohol is no longer their forté, habit. Gabriel's DUI stopped that when she fell out of the car, automobile drunk as a skunk when the police, cop pulled her over. I shave my, hairy, nubby legs almost, practically everyday for the supportive, belovéd *Gabriel* & *Dan*. Don't have a heart "attack on" me, and *please* get your own back medicine, demoral, _____ flexiril

120

from the doctor. I AM not a drug pusher, anyway. What's the deal with the lavender stenciled kitchen?

Titus & *Europe's* faithful inquiries, "How's the book going?"

Chloe & *Zachariah's* confiding, confidential, personal conversations about Jayden. Gay? Is Chickie Prickie a cover up?

"Well, *when* he gets ahold of my pussy, he won't "be" gay!" You two, *please* get married some day, tie the knot for the girls, 3 children & yourselves. I know fire & brimstone preaching is a big, damn turn-off for you all. Please "be" patient. Your awakening, special day break will come.

"We don't have a *Bible* in our house."

"I have one in almost every room."

Ecclesiastes for just being there. "You're pushing yourself too hard with the book." I look for her red cabbed truck every night.

"*When* I get some money, I want you to do some painting for me. I want the hallways a light tan, the downstairs bathroom avalon blue, and the dreaded utility, junk room avalon blue & light pink. The forbidden room needs to "be" blown off the house.

Don't say that! Mud slides & all.

I know the paint fumes do not help your alcohol problem. Hello! So what, she's gay, butch. I AM sorry about your begruged, broken relationship with *Joy*. You really shouldn't have touched her boob. I AM right in the middle of this – tugged by both sides.

St. Jude, patron of pain & suffering for being my much loved, admired comrad, pal, boss, asst. manager. "What are we going to do with all these people?"

"I saw my friend turn into a dinosaur. I was messing where I shouldn't have been messing." *What* a bond!

St. James II for being an older good buddy, nervous ready war veteran. "I love how you cross your legs." He got married, hitched later in life.

That gives me hope. "Get them young. That way you can train them the way you want them." Good idea. "We've got to quit meeting like this in the smoke room." Ha! Ha! "It's good to have your smiling face back."

"Thank you; but, I AM not smiling right now." Jebosite Haven. – "when will these bad days get better – you're the wise one."

Salvation for her soft spoken, meticulous grooming – painted fingernails, perfect mascara eyelashes, mutual, related low self esteem, lack of self-confidence.

Amos for his dry sense of humor, wit, Saint hood taking care of a severely overweight, arthritic wife in a destined wheelchair. *What* a beautiful man!

"I want to buy an orphanage, *Amos*. "Go for it!"

"What are you doing here, Mae?"

"To spread the word."

Wonderful Advisor, Counsellor: relished, treasured long distance calling, conversations; trilogy – love triangle with Brazil (Sarah Jessica Parker); married platonic old, previous boyfriend back in glory days. – cheerleading, basketball star – item, brown laid back puppy dog eyes. Thanks for believing in me. "No, I do not want to pick up a man in a bar. Those days are over."

"Let him go, Mae. He's too young for you. There are other fish in the sea. You can get a kidney transplant. They're up and walking the next day." *How* cold. *Who* runs that house, you or the cat?"

I love you; and, *always* will.

I made a mistake not keeping you.

I took the hippy road, and, you took the Jesus freak road.

Gracie Bathsheba: poor, estranged inspirational, charming scapegoat who has done numerous favors for me. One being a closer walk, stepping stone to God. Good, relilgious person deep down. Witch with black hair, green eyes & overlapping teeth. The vicious, unnessary back – stabbing, tattletelling has got to go! Sybil moods. I *love* you; but, I don't like you.

Kindness: a worthy, supportive CSM (Customer Service Manager). Shop-a-Lot could not do without her genious work ethics, control, leadership, values.

Charity: her name says it all. Her pure goodness of heart outweighs any negativity that filters through her mind, problems out of her control.

LOVED! Beautiful.

Blesséd: the GM (general merchandise) codes would never get done, organized, sorted, & put away without her diligent, hard working expertise. Her devout kindness is "tattooed on" my pulled heartstrings.

Cheer: best blood soul sister – fellow Aquarius, "born on" Valentines Day, who gets mad at me talking, conversing with Satan (sheep in wolves clothing, snake in the grass). Someone has to forgive Satan, and, it has to "be" God Himself.

Cheer's stray, wild kitties love her! She makes me laugh – "I AM going to beat you!" "Whatever!" "Please . . ."

Laughter: much, richey loved 80 years old step-Mother who raves, compliments my gifted talent, writing ability. "Do you really think so?" Chuckle. Chuckle. "Why don't you leave out the sex scenes." I don't think so. Sex sells books.

Compassion: whom I "lean on," relate, look forward to seeing her every night at Shop-a-Lot #666 #999. Dracula lover, kind head cashier. "I want to bite your neck! I want to suck your blood!"

Micah: belovéd lifelong, sweet (90% of the time) gay brother.) " This book is going to cost me $800 to publish." "You need to give up the book." You're discouragement hurts me. "Jayden will "be" there at the book signing."

Malachi: his infinite, enhancing, perplexing thoughts, information about war tactics (please, don't enlist), hillarious facial expressions, never-ending fresh loved humor.

New Guinea – big bully

Peru – little bully. "Are we in your book?" Yes, you are. I couldn't do without your funnin' about Gracie Bathsheba rolling around in her electric wheelchair, your personal problems & health issues. Give me a hug!

Isabella: constant insight, assurance, companionship, Angelic countenance & sacred gold rose cross necklace.

Royal Blue: "I was the biggest ho, whore in the community, town of Zion, Egypt."

"Oh, really, I never would have thought that."

GOD BLESS you. I AM glad you are well & alive.

Father (*GOD*), Son (*JESUS*) & Holy Spirit, Ghost (*COMFORTER*), all the Angels, Arch Angels (*CHERAPHIM, SERAPHIM*) & all the accompany of Heaven; especially *Michael*, cop, policeman guardian who saved my life from drug overdose & "where's the gun?" There is only one Arch Angel *Michael*, and I stress, emphasize that!

This *great*, wonderful celestial being can save your life, too, any day, night of the week. Call upon his name.

Thank you, *Wrangler*, my onry white cat for putting up with me ranting, raving – "Move it!", swiping, backhanding her off the cherry dining room table while I AM writing, whipping, striking her in a fit of anger for spilling, knocking over a glass of grape juice all over my brand new olive tablecloth. No, I do not believe in the belt punishing, chastising, correcting children. Wrangler thinks I AM crazy! I AM. I LOVE YOU! You furry creature.

Of course, where would I "be" without my pretty blonde, strict, positive nurse practioner, *HOPE*, whom has prevented me from dying, kicking the bucket, too many close calls, times. "You're creatin is too high! We have to do something right NOW!"

"I want quality life not quantity life. I want to "die on my Lithium.""

"Can I have a baby?"

We'll talk about that another time. Mongolism runs rapid in women over 40. Use protection. You're in good financial standing right now, Mae, *why* don't you stay the way you are." Pretty good, advise, isn't it?

Dr. Sweden: belovéd father figure; psychiatrist who saved, preserved my life by administering, prescribing Lithium. Thanks for all your hugs!

Dr. Numbers for listening, caring about all my circumstances, dilemmas, lists of problems.

Dr. Judgement: "You're a nice devil."

Dr. Glory: "You will "be" infatuated with many men – enjoy"! You live long life – enjoy! You write book after this book." and the kind, compassionate kidney physician, specialist, *Dr.*

Shepherd, whom I want to marry. He's not interested. He's married.

"How can you "be" so nice after being in the Army?"

"I AM a Nephrologist, I take blood tests."

Thank you, Bless you iUniverse, Inc. for having, welcoming me aboard.

1-800-Authors.

If I have left anyone out, *please*, God Bless your families & your friends. All your patience, support, encouragement, "egging on" will "be" paid back, reimbursed 10 fold.

It is a honor, privilege to know all this people, belovéd patron saints, and, I hopefully, reliously pray for your livelihood, eternal grace, glory including my own. Hebrew Tabernacle, Lavender Forever Church, "Rev. Elizabeth, Sarah Israel, Moses, Genesis, Job, Lazerus. "May GOD "be" with you." "And, also, with you." May all our nations rest, reside in world PEACE, one foretold, prophetized unification of competing, different walks, ways of beliefs, and may OUR Town, Zion, Egypt "live on" forever reciting, exemplifying Psalm 23.

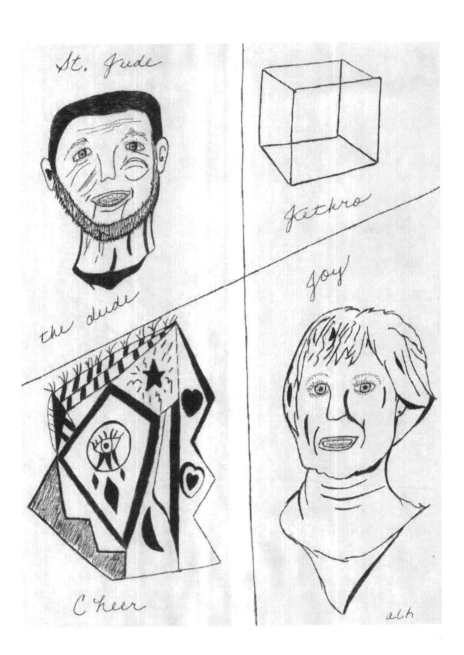

Where is Jesus's tattoo?

In the hearts and souls of humanity.

Do you know why men tattoo their dicks, penises with a $100 bill.

Because women like to blow money.

Jesus forgives you for all your infirmities, frail natures, hypocrisies.

Love & "laugh on." Are tattoos a mark of the beast or just decoration, art of the body? What do popular skulls mean?

Interpret sublime audacity.

The cross, pathway of the one Lord.

"Trod on." With blue jean sandals of "genetic love. P-E-A-C-E

All I know is, I bought a brand new pair of LEE jeans today, size 12, and they fit perfectly.

"LIVE ON"

"EXIST ON"

"LOVE ON," anyway.

Blesséd are those that trusteth, feareth the Lord, GOD.

"Trust, honor, obey Me."

"Bless on" . . .   "Abide on" . . .

                              A-M-E-N

Jeans/genes

Author Biography

Tawny "Mae" Harris resides, lives in a coal-mining, sinful, wicked, little hillbilly, redneck, hick, country town, bum ___ Zion, Egypt where people can't drive worth a SH#T in the Bible belt.

5 year cheerleader, drug addict Bicenntenial 1976 High school Graduate 1981 Associate in Art & Associate in Applied Science